NEW ENGLAND'S MOUNTAIN FLOWERS

A High Country Heritage

NEW ENGLAND'S
MOUNTAIN FLOWERS
A High Country Heritage

Jeff Wallner
Mario J. DiGregorio

IN COOPERATION WITH THE
NEW ENGLAND WILD FLOWER SOCIETY

1997
MOUNTAIN PRESS PUBLISHING COMPANY
MISSOULA, MONTANA

PRINTED IN HONG KONG BY MANTEC PRODUCTION COMPANY

Library of Congress Cataloging-in-Publication Data

Wallner, Jeff.
    New England's mountain flowers : a high country heritage / Jeff
Wallner, Mario J. DiGregorio : in cooperation with the New England
Wild Flower Society.
        p. cm.
    Includes bibliographical references (p.   ) and index.
    ISBN 0-87842-337-0 (alk. paper)
    1. Wild flowers—New England. 2. Mountain plants—New England.
3. Wild Flowers—New England—Pictorial works. 4. Mountain plants—
New England—Pictorial works. I. DiGregorio, Mario J. II. New
England Wildflower Society. III. Title.
QK121.W34 1997   97-657
582.13'0974—dc21   CIP

Mountain Press Publishing Company
P. O. Box 2399 • Missoula, MT 59806
(406) 728-1900 • (800) 234-5308

TO MARIO S. DIGREGORIO (1921–1993)
Father and Friend

❧ *Special appreciation to my parents for starting me on the road as a naturalist, and for support always. —J. W.*

❧ *Thanks to Phyllis and Sarah for providing cheerful and loving encouragement to a frequently absent husband and father. —M. J. D.*

Yellow lady's-slippers and blue wood phlox at Garden in the Woods, the New England Wild Flower Society's showcase garden and headquarters in Framingham, Massachusetts. —NEW ENGLAND WILD FLOWER SOCIETY PHOTO

NEW ENGLAND
WILD FLOWER SOCIETY

The New England Wild Flower Society is a recognized leader in native plant conservation. Founded in 1900, the Society is the oldest plant conservation organization in the United States. Its purpose is to promote the conservation of temperate North American plants through five key programs.

EDUCATION: Every year the Society teaches thousands of people of all ages and interests about native plants through courses and lectures, school programs, teachers training, tours, conferences, and field trips to fascinating habitats in New England. The Society publishes booklets and bulletins about the cultivation and propagation of native plants.

HORTICULTURE: The Society owns and operates the Garden in the Woods as its botanical garden and headquarters. As New England's premier wildflower showcase, this unique 45-acre garden is a living museum displaying the largest landscaped collection of wildflowers, ferns, shrubs, and trees in the Northeast.

RESEARCH: The Society develops economically feasible propagation techniques for native plants for the nursery industry. For private institutions and government agencies it researches the propagation and seed banking of rare and endangered species as a backup to catastrophe in the wild and for reintroduction when conditions warrant.

HABITAT PRESERVATION: The Society owns and manages seven sanctuaries in New England, protecting rare species as well as exemplary examples of New England habitats. Through various programs, the Society monitors the survival of hundreds of rare plants in the wild and assists in the preservation of rare species by providing habitat management advice and information.

CONSERVATION ADVOCACY: The Society administers the New England Plant Conservation Program, an alliance of more than 60 private organizations and public agencies working to prevent the extinction and promote the recognition of the region's endangered plants.

New England Wild Flower Society

New England Wild Flower Society
180 Hemenway Road • Framingham, MA 01701-2699
617-237-4924 • 508-877-7630
http://www.ultranet.com/~newfs/newfs.html

The New England Wild Flower Society is a nonprofit organization.

The mountains of New England,
with the location of the highest peak in each range.

CONTENTS

ACKNOWLEDGMENTS

As any field naturalist knows, one of the greatest pleasures of botanizing is the company you keep. Many people have joined us to share treasured sites or the thrill of the hunt. Thanks go to Roger Brown of the U.S. Forest Service for escorting our party to the dwarf cinquefoil on Monroe Flats; to Olivia and Doug Garfield for showing their lady's-slipper site; to Iris Baird, Joe Cabaup, and Pat Nelson at Weeks State Park for sharing our enthusiasm for purple clematis. Staff at the New England Wild Flower Society, including Bill Brumback and Frances Clark, helped with information and field trips. Fred Steele, dean of White Mountain botanists, offered expert advice to Jeff Wallner during his years at the Nature Garden.

For careful review of the text we would like to thank Frankie Brackley Tolman, adjunct professor at Keene State College and former director of the New Hampshire Natural Heritage program. In addition to her insightful comments, Frankie's superb monograph, "Orchids of New Hampshire," was especially helpful in our research. Ex-rural naturalist turned urban book dealer Gene Twaronite reviewed the text for style. He, too, is an orchid aficionado, having led us to several sites on New Hampshire Audubon's Scotland Brook Sanctuary (a gift of Gene and his wife, Jo Kelleher).

In final preparation of the text we had the expert advice of the staff at the New England Wild Flower Society, especially Barbara Pryor, Bill Brumback, Mary Walker, and Bill Cullina. Finally, to John Rimel, Kathleen Ort, and the editorial and production staff at Mountain Press, our thanks for taking words and images and molding them into a handsome book.

Cadillac Mountain summit, Acadian Hills, Maine

INTRODUCTION

MOUNTAIN FLOWERS: HISTORY AND HERITAGE

In the late nineteenth century you could stop at a Manhattan newsstand and find on the front page of the *Journal of Commerce* a list of the wildflowers in bloom in New Hampshire's White Mountains. At the height of the Gilded Era, when high society retreated to the summer comfort of the New England resorts, botanizing was one of many low-energy outdoor pursuits enjoyed by the leisure class. So, when the former editor and part owner of the *Journal*, William Cowper Prime, sent reports from his vacation suite at the Profile House, all of New York City was treated to the latest natural history news. Whether the city reader of that day paid any attention, it's intriguing for us today to imagine *The Wall Street Journal* devoting front page space to a list of flowers.

The study of New England's flowers has a long and, once, celebrated history. Naturalists were considered one of the attractions of the mountains; tourists watched for celebrity professors like Louis Agassiz or Asa Gray. Although the first settlers made little note of what they found in the mountains, unless it had some "practical" purpose, scientific parties began to explore the peaks shortly after independence. The first group to report on the vegetation of Mt. Washington consisted of three learned ministers, the Reverends Manasseh Cutler, Daniel Little, and Jeremy Belknap, representing Massachusetts, Maine, and New Hampshire. Accompanying them on this 1784 expedition was Colonel Whipple, a pioneer settler of the area west of the mountain. Their reports encouraged others, including medical doctors Jacob Bigelow and Frances Boott who, using herbs in their daily practice, were more inclined toward botanical studies than their counterparts today.

Taking to the high country from a more literary angle, naturalist-philosopher Henry Thoreau made several excursions to the White Mountains. In company with his brother, John, in 1839 he claimed to have found 42 of the 46 plant species he sought in the mountains. A later visit saw the accidental burning of an area of krummholz on Mt. Washington, neither the first

Mt. Katahdin, Longfellow Mountains, Maine

nor the last example of tourist impact on the fragile alpine environment, but ironic considering the source. Thoreau also was one of the earliest white men to climb Mt. Katahdin (or Ktaadn, as it was then spelled). On his 1846 journey, some 40 years after the first recorded ascent, he encountered a vast and alien landscape of blasted rock; his description of an hour on the summit remains a classic evocation of the netherworld of our alpine peaks.

Scientific studies on Katahdin cluster about the first few years of the twentieth century when Merritt Fernald and others combed the ridges and cirques of the grand and lonely mountain at the center of Maine. In less remote areas, the work of professionals was supported and greatly enhanced by the blossoming of the tourist trade. Mountain communities soon catered to the extravagant tastes of the well-to-do summer folk. Visiting naturalists lent their reputations to the hotels and left their names on mountain features like Oakes Gulf and Tuckerman Ravine.

Cottage colonies grew up in places like Stockbridge in the Berkshires; hotels sprawled through Manchester, Vermont, and Bethlehem, New Hampshire. Vermont claimed Brunswick Springs to be a "wonder of the world" for its cold mineral waters along the upper Connecticut River. Most famous were the hotels of the White Mountain notches: the Profile House, Crawfords, and the Mt. Washington. Access to the highest peak from the Mt. Washington hotel was made easy by the cog railroad, opened in 1869.

Each community had its coterie of knowledgeable guests who collected, pressed, and sent to regional plant collections the rare and unusual mountain flora they found on their excursions. Their enthusiasm, coupled with the proximity of botanical professionals (particularly at Harvard) made for a widespread popular knowledge of wildflowers.

With the advent of the automobile the ways of the mountain tourist began to change. It now became possible to "do the mountains" in a few days' time, carrying all one's necessities along. The Depression and the arrival of weekend tourists and middle-class leisure time hastened the demise of the grand resorts. Visitors no longer expended the time on any one place needed to gain a familiarity with the details of its natural history: tramways carried visitors far above the forests and cliffs, auto roads zipped them into and out of the alpine zone in a half-hour's time, artificial attractions and thrills replaced contemplation of nature.

Still, organizations like the Appalachian Mountain and Green Mountain Clubs kept the spirit of the pioneer naturalists alive through their publications, guided excursions, and the maintenance of mountain huts and shelters where nonharried trampers could still stop and smell the mountain daisies. Today our heritage of wildflowers is again finding a popular audience in a renewed appreciation for the quiet natural values of a varied environment. As the conservation movement found its voice, there came a call for protection of biodiversity, a concept so well represented by myriad wildflowers found in mountain habitats.

Public and private partnerships, spurred by The Nature Conservancy, have created Natural Heritage programs in each of the New England states. In addition to rediscovering the "lost" flowers recorded by the mountain visitors of a century ago, today's botanical researcher quantifies the ecological importance of the plants and advocates their protection to government officials and the public. Their efforts have brought wildflowers back to the front pages—sometimes as endangered species (like the Furbish lousewort) threatened by ill-conceived development schemes, but increasingly as indicators of the recovering health of New England's landscape.

In the spirit of the enthusiasts of the past, and in recognition of the richness wildflowers bring to our lives, we here offer our appreciation, both photographic and journalistic, of a selection of our rarest and most exquisite mountain flowers: New England's high country heritage.

GEOLOGY AND GEOGRAPHY OF MOUNTAIN FLOWERS

Theories formulated and accepted in the past 30 years have begun to make sense of 1,300 million years of landscape formation in New England. The feeling of changelessness we attribute to the mountains is misleading.

Mt. Greylock, Berkshire Mountains, Massachusetts

We must accept the geologist's view of a dynamic earth if we are to understand the forces that formed the mountains of central Maine, New Hampshire, Vermont, western Massachusetts, and Connecticut. What we see today is only the temporary product of a whole series of crustal movements, erosional episodes, collisions and riftings of continents, expansions and contractions of seas, and periodic marches of glacial ice.

Though linked geographically, our mountains have different origins, which help explain ecological distinctions. The eye easily comprehends the differing character of New Hampshire's White Mountains and Vermont's Green Mountain range; the scientific explanation is buried deep in the bedrock heart of the country. Sharing a common climate, each mountain region has its distinctive soils, hydrology, and topography reflecting the geological character; each has a prominent peak that serves to identify the range; and each has a distinctive collection of wildflowers.

Structurally, the oldest of New England's mountains are those found in the Berkshire region. The highest peaks of this province—dominated by 3,491-foot Mt. Greylock—are part of a more widespread range, the Taconics, that forms the divide between the Hudson River and Connecticut River drainages. Stretched along the New York–New England border, the Taconic Hills are found in Massachusetts, Connecticut, and Vermont.

Bedrock in the Taconics is seafloor sediment, compressed, deformed, and uplifted when an ancient ocean was caught between the oncoming American and Euro-African continents. The early movements of this 10-million-year crustal crisis—occurring about 445 million years ago—resulted in the shearing and slippage of rock layers along great thrust faults. The extent of deformation is visible in the cleavage planes of Vermont slates and Berkshire schists. The larger results are Berkshire skyline ridges.

Adding greatly to the interest of Berkshire botany is the occurrence of marble outcrops, visible in quarries along the turnpike near Stockbridge and underlying most of the valley. Marble is simply compressed limestone, and so it provides the calcium (lime) needed by many plants otherwise uncommon or rare in New England's acidic soils. The occasional occurrence of lime-bearing rocks on mountain slopes further defines a micro-habitat fit for unusual plant species.

New England's most ancient rocks occur deep within the core of Vermont's Green Mountains. The dense gneiss and quartzites found here give evidence of an ancient mountain range that dominated the landscape of an early version of North America around 1,200 million years ago. Mt. Mansfield, at 4,393 feet, is the highest of the Green Mountains, though its bedrock was moved to its present location from farther west during the faulting that formed the Taconics.

Mt. Mansfield, Green Mountains, Vermont

Accounting for the Green Mountains' elevation is the regional folding of the earth's crust, which took place during the continental collision about 335 million years ago. (One can visualize what happened to the rock layers by thinking of a loose rug on a slippery floor and how it folds when you step and push on one side.) At that time the leading edge of the old American continent became a long line of jumbled, scattered, and mashed rocks in parallel ridges and valleys trending north and south—the definition of Vermont's landscape.

Another result of the ancient collision of continents was the formation of molten rock within the earth—the same process we see today where India and Asia meet as the Himalayas. Some of this emerged as lava flows, forming a line of offshore volcanic islands much like today's Japan. Caught between the continents, these rocks were welded onto America and appear as a line of hills along the "suture zone," approximated by the Connecticut River valley between New Hampshire and Vermont.

Other areas of these Connecticut River uplands consist of molten rock that cooled underground to form granite bodies, or of seafloor sediments scraped up during the closing of that ancient sea. Differences in the structure

Mt. Monadnock, Connecticut River uplands, New Hampshir

and composition of these rocks result in erosion leaving more resistant peaks standing above the river valley. Monadnock Mountain (3,145 feet) in southwestern New Hampshire is a typical example, but other monadnocks include Vermont's own Monadnock (in the Northeast Kingdom) and Mt. Ascutney. Southward, sedimentary rocks of the Mt. Holyoke range stand high above the current erosional plain of the river, their sandstones remnants of earlier mountain ranges.

At about the same time that the Green Mountains were folded upward, large, dome-shaped masses of molten material rose up into the bedrock of what was to become the state of Maine. These granite intrusions of approximately 375 million years ago now form the resistant summits of the state's two most celebrated mountains: Cadillac Mountain (1,530 feet) in the coastal Acadian Hills and Mt. Katahdin (5,267 feet) in the heart of Baxter State Park. Erosion led to the uncovering of these granite peaks; elevation has kept Katahdin in the alpine zone, whereas rugged coastal weather and periodic fires give Cadillac its rocky look.

Although Katahdin stands far from any other high peaks, it marks the northeastern end of a line of mountains referred to on maps as the Longfellow Mountains, popularly ascribed to the vast region called The Maine Woods. Backbone of this region and host to the wildest stretches of the Appalachian Trail, these peaks—Bigelow, Sugarloaf, Saddleback, Old Speck—share geological and botanical affinities with the White Mountains.

At 6,288 feet, Mt. Washington, or Agiochook as the Abenaki call it, dominates New England's landscape and imagination: it was once thought to be the highest mountain in North America. The structure of Mt. Washington is similar to Monadnock's: a resistant down-warp in a compressed seafloor sediment called schist. Thus, ironically, neither of the Granite State's most famous mountains is made of granite.

Surrounding peaks and terrain in the White Mountains are dominated by granite or related rocks, making up the cores of the Franconia and Ossipee ranges, Cannon Mountain, and Chocorua. Signifying an invasion of molten rock domes into the region about 175 million years ago, these White Mountain formations mark the beginning of a great breakup of the continents, which slowly led to the global configuration we know today. Thus, the White Mountains are structurally New England's youngest, bearing scant topographic resemblance to the older, western ranges.

In addition to covering the mountains of New England, this book provides an overview of the wildflowers of New York's Adirondack Mountains. A granite range of independent geological origin, the Adirondacks harbor the only alpine areas in the northeast outside of New England. In this way they resemble the White Mountains, while lower reaches of the

Mt. Washington, White Mountains, New Hampshire

sprawling Adirondack Park are home to plants more typical of Vermont's Green Mountains.

All of New England looks as it does today because millions of years of erosion have shaped the bedrock. Most notable to us is the action of continent-wide glaciers, which covered all of the mountains with a two-mile-thick layer of ice until only 14,000 years ago. Melted away, ice age glaciers left behind smoothed slopes and sheer cliffs, rugged talus slopes and slick ledges, long gravelly eskers, rocky hillside soils, rich lakeshore deposits, and barren alpine areas—the very places where the plant communities of modern New England, explored in the following chapters, could grow and thrive.

How to Use This Book

New England's Mountain Flowers: A High Country Heritage is meant to be an appreciative look at wildflowers, an exploration of plant lore, and a plea for their protection. It is *not* meant as a comprehensive field guide in any sense of the word. Of the hundreds of species of wildflowers in the five mountainous states of New England, only 85 are covered here. We recommend two field guides to supplement this work: *Newcomb's Wildflower Guide* and the Appalachian Mountain Club's *Field Guide to Mountain Flowers of New England*.

Some of our showiest native mountain species can be found here simply by flipping the pages. But we have focused much of our attention on the rarer flowers, which the casual observer is unlikely to encounter. Also, we have included only a handful of examples of introduced species. These botanical settlers dominate the wildflower scene around human structures—particularly highways—and are to be the subject of a later volume on roadside wildflowers.

The book is arranged in chapters based on habitat types. All flowers have preferences for certain soils, exposures, and climates. Some cross borders and inhabit several different environments. However, more so than other species, our rarest wildflowers tend to have specific habitat requirements. If using this guide for identification, turn first to the chapter that best describes the surroundings in which you found the flower.

Each plant's essay appears directly opposite a full-color picture of the flower. One or more common names are given, followed by a scientific name of Greek or Latin origin. This name consists of the genus name, shared by closely related plants, and the specific epithet (species name) for that kind of flower. Species are variable in appearance depending on genetics and growth conditions, and the botanical understanding of the species concept allows for hybridization. Details of these variations from the norm are included in the text. Scientific names in this book follow the nomenclature of *A Synonymized Checklist of Vascular Flora of the United States, Canada, and Greenland* by John and Rosemarie Kartesz.

The text explores the lore of the flower in both natural and human history and describes threats to its continued existence where pertinent. Interesting derivations of plant names are explored and descriptions of plant ecology and "behavior" are given. At the end of each entry we include information on the habitat, rarity, and flowering time of the wildflowers.

Photographs were taken at wild stations within the region by the authors using Canon and Nikon equipment, with macro, conventional, and wide-angle lenses and Kodak Ektachrome and Fujichrome film.

White birch forest, New Hampshire

FOREST SLOPES

From a hawk's perch on an open ledge the New England mountains appear as a green sea; vibrant where hardwoods dominate but deeper and more inscrutable where conifers cloak the heights. These differences in shading conveniently define the dynamic transition between northern hardwood and coniferous forest types that lends drama to our mountainsides.

The forest flora of the Appalachians is spectacular in its variety and lushness from the Gaspé to the foothill ranges of Alabama and Georgia. Oddly enough, these mountain forests have affinities to those of the Pacific Northwest and central Asia. Rhododendrons, trilliums, woodland lilies, and wood sorrels are a component of each of these communities, though they are absent in the drier forests of the Rocky Mountains. There is a feeling of antiquity about these forests; indeed the magnolia family of the southern Appalachians is considered among the most primitive of flowering plants.

The physical aspect of mountain forests that most immediately affects wildflowers is the predominance of shade from the trees above. In the hardwood forest there is a brief season, after killing frosts but before full leafing, when the forest floor is both warm and flush with light. In this season, measured in days rather than months, a host of plants puts forth leaves, buds, flowers, and fruit in a rush to seed—a prodigal burst of photosynthetic energy before leaf cover shuts out the energy-rich sunlight. There are so many of these flowers, in such a variety of families, that they have been given the collective name of spring ephemerals for their here-today-gone-tomorrow lifestyle.

Shade and acidity characterize the forest soils of the coniferous forest. Here wildflowers spread wide leaves to maximize the capture of light, as in lady's-slippers, or have no photosynthesizing leaves at all, as in pinedrops and coralroots. Breaks in the forest canopy where sunlight steals to the earth provide space for clumps of bunchberry dogwood. Cold, moist, shaded soils sprout plants like goldthread, twinflower, dewdrop, and mountain shamrock. Hardy, often evergreen, sprawling and spreading by runners, these are the elfin wildflowers of the northern forest.

Richer soils underlie the hardwood forests. In western New England especially the soils are enriched with lime, allowing calcium-loving flowers like squirrel corn, white trillium, toothwort, and wild ginger to thrive. In the southern hills the flora of the Blue Ridge range of Virginia and the Carolinas make their most northerly stands. Look to the Berkshires and Taconics for species like showy orchis, great rhododendron, and mayapple. These are the species, north of their usual haunts, restricted to lime-bearing rock and soil formations in acidic country, that are some of New England's rarest mountain flowers, worth long trips and tramps into the wooded countryside.

Climate and soils are not the only limiting factors on the variety of our wildflower heritage. In the south we are losing habitat at an alarming rate to second home development, while in the north we continue to see changes in the balance of forest types due to centuries of human intervention and management. Throughout the region we encounter the uncertainties of global warming and acid precipitation. Some predictions set the future range of the sugar maple somewhere north of New England! Our wildflower mosaic is a result of eons of compromise and change in natural systems. Sudden alterations by humans will have the greatest effect on those species with the least natural resistance to change, those plants that are already naturally rare.

BUNCHBERRY or DWARF CORNEL
Cornus canadensis

This handsome little "dwarf" guides the hiker up cool forested trails to well above tree line. A member of the distinctive dogwood family, the bunchberry is an herb, unlike the trees and shrubs that make up the vast majority of dogwoods.

Bunchberry rises from a creeping woody rhizome to a height of 6 to 7 inches at lower elevations, struggling to 2 to 3 inches at or above timberline. The characteristic ovate dogwood leaves are paired on the stem in what appear to be two-tiered whorls. Actually, the four to six leaves are spaced very close to the stem, giving a whorl-like appearance.

Like the flowering dogwood *(Cornus florida)*, the so-called flower petals of bunchberry are actually modified leaves called bracts. Four of these white or pink-tinged bracts surround the tiny, yellow-and-black flowers crowded in the center of the head.

Bunchberry gets its name from the brilliant red fruit crowded atop the stem. A walker headed up a mountain trail in late July will see this plant in plump fruit at lower elevations; as one ascends, the calendar reverses itself. At midelevations the bunchberry shows immature green fruit at this time, and is back freshly in flower above timberline as late as August. For this reason, fruiting bunchberry is rare at high elevations.

While bunchberry fruit is hardly a taste treat, it is also known as puddingberry, probably because of a closely related species, which is extensively used in Lapland and Scandinavia in the making of a pudding dessert.

Habitat: *Cool forests and slopes*
Flowers: *May to early August*
Status: *Common*

Bunchberry flower   *Cornus canadensis*

Bunchberry fruit   *Cornus canadensis*

TWINFLOWER
Linnaea borealis ssp. *americana*

While any natural history writer attempts to shy away from descriptions of "delicate" and "lovely" in order to spare the reader from mind-numbing clichés, it simply must be said: The twinflower is among the loveliest, most delicate of northern forest wildflowers. (Fernald gushingly calls it "a pretty little plant" in *Gray's Manual of Botany*.)

Creeping almost unnoticed in mossy, cool forests in most of northern New England, this diminutive evergreen must be examined closely to be truly appreciated.

Rising 3 to 4 inches above the paired roundish leaves, its sparsely hairy stem branches into two equal pedicels. White to dark pink trumpet-shaped blossoms hang pendulously from each stalk, with five flaring corolla lobes emitting the most delicious fragrance (a trait shared by other members of the honeysuckle family).

The perfect symmetry and grace of the plant is a joy to behold. The flowers seem mirror images of each other, so much so that the species was known colloquially as twin sisters.

Flowering in June and July at most elevations in boreal woodlands, twinflower occasionally grows into the krummholz zone as high as 5,000 feet, where it blooms in late summer. It ranges over the northern half of North America, as well as Europe and Asia.

The most well-known portrait of Carolus Linnaeus, the father of modern plant taxonomy, shows the famed botanist lovingly holding a sprig of twinflower, his personal favorite. His protégé, Gronovius, dedicated the plant to Linnaeus by naming the genus after him. Linnaeus had this to say about the plant: "[twinflower] is a plant of Lapland lowly, insignificant, disregarded, flowering but for a brief space, after Linnaeus, who resembles it."

Habitat: *Occasional in cool, mossy woods*
Flowers: *June or July*
Status: *Fairly common; Watch List species in Massachusetts*

Twinflower   *Linnaea borealis* ssp. *americana*

STARFLOWER
Trientalis borealis

Spring ephemerals are those wildflowers that bloom for a short period in midspring before the leaf canopy shuts out the sunlight from the forest floor. They are usually white or a light pastel and are gone long before we're ready to bid them adieu.

One of the best-known and most eagerly awaited of these spring wonders is the starflower or May-star.

Spreading by stolons or runners, starflower sometimes carpets an undisturbed woodland in a solid bed of dark green leaves and vivid white flowers. Starflower is named for its seven-pointed gossamer blossom, which positively sparkles if the sunlight is strongly reflected off the diamond-shaped petals or if a breeze moves the tremulous heads on their threadlike stalks.

It is one of the few wildflowers to have its floral parts arranged in sevens; seven petals, seven stamens, and usually even seven seeds within the capsule! The genus name *Trientalis* refers to another aspect of the plant: its height of about a third of a foot.

New Englanders are fortunate to be blessed with good numbers of starflowers throughout the region. Found wherever there are moist, cool woodlands, this species ascends as high as alpine elevations. Across the Atlantic, wildflower fanciers are not so lucky; a national park in Germany is named Trientalis National Park, in honor of the beautiful but seldom seen European variety.

Habitat: *Rich woodlands*
Flowers: *May to early June*
Status: *Common*

Starflower *Trientalis borealis*

BLUEBEAD LILY
Clintonia borealis

Natural historians trade tales, and one of our favorites tells of a woman we met in the woods with a hatful of "blueberries" that she had picked from convenient long stalks poking up from the forest floor. Her obvious delight in this treasure trove shut out any thought of disillusioning her, and we trust that she found out, with a taste of these insipid fruits, that the bluebead lily deserves its reputation among New England youngsters as an inedible "snakeberry."

The berries are certainly the most visible feature of this plant, for the three to eight clustered, greenish yellow flowers face downward and tend to blend in with the other greenery of late May. Besides the confusion of berries, the ovate basal leaves are reminiscent of those of the pink lady's-slipper, and grow in similar habitats. The bluebead's leaf lacks the orchid's prominent ribbed veins, and it is more apt to appear in sprawling colonies, spreading by its rootstocks.

Examined on bended knee the plant exhibits characteristics of the more well-known lilies: six petals, stamens and pistils exserted from the corolla; parallel-veined leaves; and fruit in form of a fleshy and porcelain blue (save for the white bead of form *albicarpa*) capsule. A plant of moist woods and upland terrain, the genus *Clintonia* is represented in the southern Appalachians (by a lanky, white-flowered species), in the redwood forests (by a red-flowered form), and in similar habitats in Asia.

The name *Clintonia* honors New York governor DeWitt Clinton, better known as the chief promoter of the Erie Canal. Like many successful public figures of the nineteenth century, Clinton pursued natural history in addition to his public duties. Many field guides use this rather sonorous Latin name as a common name, avoiding the plethora of English names for this typical mountain forest plant: corn lily, straw lily, bead lily, and cow tongue.

Habitat: *All regions—forests to timberline*
Flowers: *May and June*
Status: *Common*

Bluebead Lily *Clintonia borealis*

WILD GINGER
Asarum canadense

Wild ginger is a curious little plant of calcareous woodland slopes. Its broadly heart-shaped and aromatic rootstocks are more distinctive than the brown-red flower, which skulks close to the ground, often covered with forest duff.

The pungent, spicy root was long used by settlers and Native Americans alike as both a pharmaceutical and food. European settlers called it Canadian snakeroot, after its thick, sinuous rhizome, which adds a segment with each year's growth. Chippewa Indians called it sturgeon plant and used it similarly.

Overcollected in the nineteenth century for use as a digestive aid and a spice, wild ginger became "very scarce" in the words of one herbal guide published in 1906. The writer of that guide goes on to complain of the exorbitant price of 10 to 15 cents a pound for wild gingerroot. At those rates, it's little wonder the plant became uncommon.

Nibbling the jointed taproot is not for the faint of heart; a "ginger snap gone ballistic" is how one botanist describes it.

Ranging from Vermont south to the Appalachian Mountains of North Carolina and west to Kansas, wild ginger is a polymorphous species, once thought to comprise three separate species before being lumped into *Asarum canadense*. It is not the commercially sold gingerroot; that well-known spice is Asian in origin and is not related to our wild ginger.

A reasonably alert walker in late April can usually find wild ginger beneath an oak or beech canopy in limestone areas. The two heart-shaped leaves mark the plant's presence; the shy flower is slung face down between them and is commonly covered over with dead leaves and humus. Its hidden aspect and ill scent attract furtive visitors like fungus gnats, ground beetles, and flesh flies, unlikely and unlovely agents of cross-pollination.

Habitat: *Rocky, calcareous woods*
Flowers: *April to May*
Status: *Fairly common*

Wild Ginger   *Asarum canadense*

YELLOW LADY'S-SLIPPER OR
YELLOW MOCCASIN FLOWER
Cypripedium parviflorum and *C. pubescens*

This elegant lady's-slipper comes in two sizes; large *(Cypripedium pubescens)* and small *(C. parviflorum)*. While closely resembling each other (some writers consider them varieties of the same species), they can be distinguished, both by appearance and habitat.

The small yellow slipper grows in swampy woods, chiefly in calcareous or limy soil. The pouch or slipper color is a deep, almost luminescent yellow with a kind of waxy veneer. Adorning the slipper are madder purple petals and sepals, which appear twisted or contorted into braids. The blossom is strongly fragrant. Late May to early July is the best time to look for this 22- to 24-inch-tall orchid.

The large species grows to 3 feet in height, usually in rocky woods with rich but not necessarily wet soil. While the intense yellow of the flower can be startling in the filtered shade of its habitat, it is not quite as vivid a hue as the small yellow. The petals are greenish yellow and not as twisted. It also lacks the pleasant fragrance of *C. parviflorum*. The large yellow species most often flowers earlier in May than its diminutive relation.

The great beauty of lady's-slippers did not prevent the wholesale destruction of this species at the turn of the century by root collectors, who sold the thick rhizomes as a pharmaceutical.

Marketed as "nerve-root" and "male nervine," the plant was thought to have superior qualities as a sedative and nerve tonic, and was popular for this use well into the 1920s. For the princely sum of 32 cents a pound for the root, the enchanting slipper of Aphrodite, goddess of love, was nearly wiped out.

While both small- and large-flowered yellows are still occasionally seen in large colonies, they remain rare and local in most of our region today. Generally, the large-flowered species is far more frequent.

Habitat (large): *Rocky wooded slopes*
Habitat (small): *Calcareous swamps*
Flowers: *Late May to early July*
Status: *Rare; threatened (large) and endangered (small) species in New Hampshire; Watch List species in Vermont (both) and Massachusetts (large)*

Large Yellow
Lady's-Slipper
Cypripedium pubescens

Small Yellow Lady's-Slipper   *Cypripedium parviflorum*

GREAT ROSEBAY
Rhododendron maximum

Representative mountain flower of the southern Appalachians, great rosebay or great laurel struggles to its northern limit in New England. Though its mountainside occurrences here are limited to the Berkshires and Taconics, it grows in sheltered valleys among the hills, as near Mt. Monadnock and in the Green Mountains.

Scattered stations of this spectacular white-blossomed rhododendron are found throughout the region. To the north, Maine lists 7 locations (several designated as critical habitat areas), New Hampshire lists 12, and Vermont 9, including one in Troy on the Canadian border. Relicts of a warmer time, these colonies cling to existence in swampy kettle holes, moist shaded forests, and along pond shores. Rhododendron State Park in Fitzwilliam, New Hampshire, and Groton State Forest in Vermont are excellent places to see wild colonies of a plant not often associated with northern New England.

Rhododendrons and azaleas of this genus are among the world's favorite cultivated shrubs, with some hybrids producing nauseatingly gaudy displays. Such garden sports are often crosses between the hardy American species and more colorful Himalayan varieties. In general the name *azalea* is given to those species with swept-back petals and exerted stamens, while *rhododendron*—Greek for "rose tree"—applies to those species with cup-shaped flowers in big, snowball clusters.

At least as interesting, whether in the garden or in the wild, are the rosebay's inch-long, leathery evergreen leaves. These serve as a natural thermometer for those who have the shrub about their homes. The leaves respond to cold by rolling up into ever tighter cylinders as the temperature drops. To gauge the day's temperature, just remember that the tighter the roll, the colder the day.

Rhododendrons thrive in acidic situations and are thus suited to our mountain soils, if not our mountain winters. In healthy clumps, as in the Connecticut highlands, the shrubs grow nearly to tree size of 30 feet and bloom around the Fourth of July—a natural alternative to fireworks displays.

Habitat: *Widely scattered in damp areas*
Flowers: *Early July*
Status: *Rare and possibly declining*

Great Rosebay   *Rhododendron maximum*

FOAMFLOWER or FALSE MITERWORT
Tiarella cordifolia

After the first wave of spring ephemerals such as bloodroot and hepatica have come and gone, rich woodland floors are often covered in a carpet of brilliant foamflowers after forest canopy closure.

A 6- to 8-inch raceme of snow-white flowers with long, filamentous stamens topped with chunky yellow or orange anthers characterizes this attractive member of the saxifrage family. The basal leaves arise separately from the rhizome and somewhat resemble miniature maple leaves.

The distinctive seed capsule gives the plant both its genus and English names. Splitting in two, it appears to resemble a small crown or tiara, hence *Tiarella*; it's also been compared to a bishop's miter, thus accounting for false miterwort. Gem-fruit is yet another popular name alluding to the seed shape.

Whereas foamflower will not grow higher than tree line in New England, it has been found to 6,000 feet in the Smoky Mountains.

Wherever encountered, the effervescent foamflower represents spring at its acme, and for this alone it is a welcome sight.

Habitat: *Rich, acidic woods*
Flowers: *May to June*
Status: *Common*

Foamflower or False Miterwort *Tiarella cordifolia*

WAKEROBIN or RED TRILLIUM
Trillium erectum

PAINTED TRILLIUM
Trillium undulatum

The painted trillium, so common in New England's mountain forests, grows nearly to timberline, while the wakerobin, that royal purple banner of spring, grows in lower forests. Both have a long floral history leading to the appearance of their three-petaled flowers.

The trillium life story begins inside a shiny red berry borne on the mature plant stalk. After this capsule splits open and the seeds fall to the ground they are likely to be collected by ants that feed on the fuzzy strophiole attached to each seed. Discarded by the ants, the seed itself germinates in suitably moist soil, then takes up to six years to come to flower, overwintering as a rootstalk and putting out progressively larger leaves each year. In its youth the plant is more likely to have one or two leaf parts rather than the three leaves of the flowering plant.

The length of time to flowering cannot be speeded up and so trilliums are notoriously difficult to propagate. In fact, the New England Wild Flower Society, in an attempt to discourage purchases of plants dug from the wild, has issued a caution to its members. Pointing out that "trillium propagation is slow, generally inefficient, and consequently expensive," the society warns against any dealer offering large numbers of cheap trilliums; they are most likely dug up from the wild.

Trilliums characterize the Appalachian flora, yet folk uses are few. There are records of eating the young shoots in salads, but this practice generally destroys the underground plant. In the South, where more species exist, some have been used in midwifery and carry the name birthroot. A glance at the three-leaved, three-petaled, three-sepaled plants makes the name *Trillium* seem quite sufficient. Still, those who tire of the ordinary can seek out teratological varieties of either species of trillium. In painted trillium, for example, there is form *polymerum* with four to eight parts—leaves, sepals, petals—rather than the usual three. *Gray's Manual of Botany* even talks about "exceptional plants" with two leaves and two petals. Imagine a springtime hunt for di-illiums, quadrilliums, or even octilliums!

Habitat (Painted trillium): *Upland forests and swamps*
Habitat (Wakerobin): *Rich woods*
Flowers: *May and June*
Status: *Both common, but subject to overcollection*

Wakerobin or Red Trillium
Trillium erectum

Painted Trillium   *Trillium undulatum*

DEWDROP
Dalibarda repens

Antique botany texts have a delightful mixture of the precisely scientific and the poetic. Take this description of *Dalibarda* from Asa Gray's 1895 *Field, Forest, and Garden Botany* as revised by Liberty Hyde Bailey: "A low, stemless, tufted, downy, little plant, spreading more or less by subterranean runners, with the aspect of a violet, the scapes bearing 1 or 2 delicate white flowers, in summer." The strings of adjectives and defining phrases demonstrate a peculiar affection for the finest details of the plant.

Dewdrop, also known as false violet and by the intriguing name robin-run-away, is the sole member of its genus, thought to be closely related to blackberries. The scientific name honors Thomas Francois Dallibard, a Parisian botanist known to Linnaeus and his assistant Peter Kalm. They named this native American plant during their work on pressed specimens in a European laboratory, a common practice during the formative days of plant taxonomy.

A late bloomer for the dark woods of the New England mountains, where most flowering takes place in spring, dewdrop flowers are unexpected flashes of white in damp, shady places. The flowers contrast brightly against the evergreen leaves that trail over the ground in spreading clumps. Each flower has a spray of silky stamens with yellow tips, typical of members of the rose family. Yet this noticeable flower has little useful purpose, for dewdrop is one of those plants in which self-pollination is the rule.

The showy, five-petaled flowers that we value for their daintiness are generally sterile; they do not produce seeds. Instead, below these infertile flowers, on smaller, curled-back stems, are flowers that do not open until ripe. Inside these closed (cleistogamous) flowers the anthers and stigmas remain in close contact, and the plant is pollinated without the interference of prying insects. Only later, when the dry seedlike fruit breaks out of the closed sepals does this flower open to its environment, with a small chance that its seeds will be moved to a new location to parent a clump of *Dalibarda* leaves.

Habitat: *Damp montane forests and bogs*
Flowers: *July and early August*
Status: *Fairly common in northern New England*

Dewdrop   *Dalibarda repens*

DUTCHMAN'S BREECHES
Dicentra cucullaria

SQUIRREL CORN
Dicentra canadensis

Here are two spring woodland flowers that have long captured the imagination of naturalists. The quaint name Dutchman's breeches harkens back to the puffy pantaloons of Hudson River valley settlers. The racemes of white flowers *do* look like a row of these garments hung out to dry, at least after the name has conjured up the image.

Squirrel corn too has a memorable name, though the responsible feature is not so conspicuous. Only on the underground runners of the plant will you find the bright yellow grains that lead to the name. Because this plant is considered rare in several New England states (and may not exist at all in Maine), we strongly urge that you take our word for this aspect, as we have taken the word of other botany texts.

Plants in the fumitory family are closely related to those in the poppy family, but they lack the colored poisonous sap of that group and have far more imaginative flowers. Each *Dicentra* blossom is composed of two pairs of petals—each member of the pair having a different shape from the other. The result is a number of unusual forms: breeches, bleeding hearts (squirrel corn flowers are pale hearts), ear drops, and even a steer's skull.

The six pollen-bearing stamens and single pistil stick out from between the petals, one of which forms a cup-shaped spur, depository of a nectar droplet. Bumblebees reach in with their long tongues to tap this rich source of natural sugars, and in the process gather quantities of pollen on their heads for transport to the next flower. Tiny, round, hard seeds (like poppy seeds) in dry capsules are the ultimate result.

Both of these flowers are up-country dwellers, extending down the Appalachian Mountains to Georgia. Dutchman's breeches also occur in an isolated patch of the Oregon and Washington Cascades. Of the two species, squirrel corn is far less common, and more likely to be found in limy areas; both are most common in the Connecticut River watershed.

Habitat (Dutchman's breeches): *Woods, lower mountain slopes*
Flowers: *April and May*
Status: *Occasional, more frequent in north*

Habitat (Squirrel Corn): *Rich woods, lower slopes*
Flowers: *April and May*
Status: *Uncommon to rare (in New Hampshire and Maine)*

Dutchman's Breeches   *Dicentra cucullaria*

Squirrel Corn   *Dicentra canadensis*

SPRING BEAUTY
Claytonia caroliniana

The limp, succulent, and sprightly spring beauties were given their scientific name in honor of one of America's earliest botanical explorers, John Clayton, who contributed plant material for an early flora of Virginia. In bestowing common names on our two species of *Claytonia* the names Virginia and Carolina are often used. This can be misleading to those who know their geography and assume that the Virginia spring beauty occurs farther north than the Carolina. Just the opposite is true.

Although a smaller plant than *Claytonia virginica*, our mountain spring beauty shares its pink, purple-veined flowers, two persistent sepals, and paired leaves halfway up the stem. The northern species' leaves are much wider than the southern, so it has been called broader leaf spring beauty. In New England, *C. virginica* is rare in low elevations; *C. caroliniana* is the mountain plant of open hardwood forests. Found in the Berkshires, throughout Vermont, in northern New Hampshire, and western Maine, a few plants even make it above timberline, as in Oakes Gulf, on Mt. Washington. Alpine and montane species of *Claytonia* are quite common in the western mountains of North America, whereas others are found as far away as New Zealand and Australia.

The spring beauty presents one of the earliest of color shows in the woods. Locally in the White Mountains distinctive drops of pale pink adorn insignificant green stems amid piles of tan beech and maple leaves in late April. Later, large colonies spread pink-white carpets in certain choice locales—the col between Artist Bluff and Bald Peak in Franconia Notch is a personal favorite.

The flowering stalks of spring beauty rise from an enlarged underground stem or corm, which gastronomical botanist Euell Gibbons referred to as fairy spuds. Widely reported to have been a common food source for natives and colonists, the ½- to 2-inch corms are usually boiled and eaten peeled, the flavor said to resemble chestnuts or potatoes. Like many members of the purslane family, the leafy parts can be used as a potherb or added to salads. After his enthusiastic description of eating a large batch of these plants (which made way for a cultivated garden) Gibbons suggested restraint in gathering a plant that is "food for the soul."

Habitat: *Rich, open woods and slopes*
Flowers: *May (June in alpine)*
Status: *Uncommon, but populations well established*

Spring Beauty   *Claytonia caroliniana*

WILD SARSAPARILLA
Aralia nudicaulis

Although not directly related to the sarsaparilla used to flavor the old soda-fountain favorite, the aromatic root of this plant has been touted as a temperate zone alternative. The original version, a tropical American plant, was named *zarza parra* or "bramble vine" by the Spanish, and was used to impart a pungent flavor to the carbonated drink. A generic substitute with the same flavor is available in your neighborhood drugstore—the montane forests of New England.

The Araliaceae or ginseng family has few representatives in the United States, though there is a great deal of variety in the species we have. Most celebrated is the ginseng, hunted to near extermination in the eastern mountains by herb collectors who got top dollar for the medicinal root. More familiar is the cultivated English ivy, an example of the vine growth form in the family, imported from Europe for its decorative leaves. The tallest and most formidable of the *Aralias* is the Hercules club or devil's walking stick, a spiny tree with just the mien that its common names evoke.

Wild sarsaparilla is not armed with the bristles of its cousins *Aralia spinosa* and *A. hispida* (the latter species is sometimes found on dry roadsides in the New England mountains). The species name means "naked stalk" and refers not to the smoothness but to the lack of leaves on the flower stalk. The leaf stalk with three-part compound leaves rises separately on a longer stem, shading the flowers. Taken singly the greenish white flowers are unimpressive, but they grow in round umbels with many blooms and prominent stamens, which give the inflorescence the exuberant aspect of holiday fireworks, at least to the close-up lens!

Not immediately apparent to the flower observer is the tough, reclining woody stem of wild sarsaparilla. Perennial and barely rising above the ground, the stem is the bane of anyone attempting to establish a trail in our mountain forests. An area that in fall or early spring appeared to be clear of vegetation will sprout colonies of gangly leaved sarsaparilla to reclaim the path for summer's green.

Habitat: *Primarily hardwood forests, below 4,000 feet*
Flowers: *June*
Status: *Common*

Wild Sarsaparilla *Aralia nudicaulis*

LARGE-FLOWERED BELLWORT
Uvularia grandiflora

A spring pilgrimage never to be missed is a late April or early May visit to the New England Wild Flower Society sanctuary in Plainfield, New Hampshire. There, on the road below the rich wooded slopes, the eyes can feast on a panoply of color from Dutchman's breeches, red trillium, miterwort, squirrel corn, trout lily, toothwort, and long-spurred violet. This is the dazzling display of the so-called spring ephemerals, wildflowers that quickly blossom before the leaf canopy of the forest trees shades out the sun. These delicate species seem to appear overnight only to vanish for another year, almost before we've had the chance to admire them.

Appearing on the heels of the first wave of April flowers is the large-flowered bellwort. This spring specialty seems to be perpetually drooping, hanging its head in a vain attempt to hide its subtle beauty. With long, slightly twisted petals held in a partially closed position, big merry-bells appears never to be fully in bloom.

The lance-shaped leaves are perfoliate, meaning they actually surround the stem rather than attach at one point as with most plants. This feature is characteristic of other species of bellwort, of which there are four in New England. At 2 feet in height, large-flowered bellwort is indeed the largest of the bellworts. Unlike the paler members of the genus, this species has lemon yellow flowers that droop pendulously above the forked stem. This drooping visage gives the entire genus its name Uvularia, from "uvula," the hanging flap of flesh behind the mouth's soft palate.

Large-flowered bellwort is widely distributed but nowhere truly abundant. It ranges from Ontario and Quebec south through New England to the mountains of Tennessee and Georgia. It prefers well-drained, chiefly calcareous soils on steep to moderate slopes in rich woodlands.

Old botanical manuals swear by a Colonial-era poultice made from the leaves and flowers used to remedy toothache. Its medicinal value was well known to New England's indigenous population, which used a root tea to alleviate a whole host of rheumatic pains and fevers.

Habitat: *Wooded, calcareous slopes*
Flowers: *Late April to early May*
Status: *Uncommon to rare; endangered species in Connecticut and New Hampshire (not reported from Maine)*

Large-Flowered Bellwort *Uvularia grandiflora*

MOUNTAIN SHAMROCK
Oxalis acetosella ssp. *montana*

Children who join us on explorations of the north country woods recognize the cloverlike leaves of the mountain shamrock and relate them to the weedy, yellow-flowered *Oxalis* plants that grow around their homes. The children's name for both plants is sour grass, but wood sorrel is the name applied to all members of the mostly tropical family (in the tropics some genera are shrubs or small trees and have edible fruit) to which this plant belongs.

The name *sorrel* is used for plants of otherwise unrelated families that have sour or acidic-flavored foliage. In fact the scientific name for this species, *acetosella*, means "little vinegar plant." Both mountain shamrock and *Rumex acetosella*, the sheep sorrel, are suggested as flavor enhancers for wild salads.

The oxalic acid, which gives the bite to the leaves of mountain shamrock, is derived from calcium oxalate, a cellular substance that is believed to assist in the maintenance of pH balance within the leaves. The sharp oxalate crystals can be distressing to the digestive tract, so eating large quantities is not suggested. But a nip of sour grass leaf can add flavor to any woodland ramble.

Seen without their flowers, patches of mountain shamrock leaves, spread by underground runners, are a cheerful sight in the shade of coniferous forests. Blooming in midsummer, the five-petaled white flowers are striped with rosy lines, which are brilliant nectar guides when seen in the wavelengths of bee vision. Often these are the only flowers to be found in the woods during that interregnum between the spring ephemerals and the fall asters. Purple-flowered plants of this species found in New England are known as form *rhodantha*; the violet species, which has clusters rather than single flowers, does not occur in New England's mountains.

Although the flowers are showy and, through cross-pollination, provide for evolutionary flexibilty, they are actually less likely to set seed than are the self-pollinating flowers, which appear on separate stems at the same time of year. Either way, the plant develops a compact seed capsule that opens explosively when ripe, sprinkling seed away from the parent colony of "shamrock" leaves.

Habitat: *Damp, chiefly coniferous forests*
Flowers: *June to August*
Status: *Common in northern New England, uncommon in southern New England*

Mountain Shamrock *Oxalis acetosella* ssp. *montana*

MOUNTAIN LAUREL
Kalmia latifolia

This impressive flowering shrub is neither a true laurel nor particularly prevalent on mountains in New England. It prefers low-lying acidic rocky woods, where it can form pure stands of impenetrable thickets 20 to 30 feet high.

Mountain laurel presents a stately sight in the latter half of June with great corymbs of pink to white parasol-shaped flowers contrasting with the dark, leathery evergreen leaves.

A closer look at the flower reveals ten trigger-loaded stamens, anthers securely restrained in ten pits within the corolla until a drop of rain or a bumblebee comes along to spring the stamens free. Two terminal pores in the anthers release a cobwebby kind of pollen that ensnares the nectar-seeking bee. The pollen then may come in contact with the stigma of the next blossom the unwitting "mule" visits, increasing the chances of cross-pollination.

Mountain laurel ranges from Maine to Florida, attaining its greatest size of nearly 40 feet high in the mid-Atlantic states. It was known in the nineteenth century as spoonwood because of its close-grained, hard wood, which nonetheless carved easily into a variety of wooden implements such as spoons, ladles, and bowls.

As with other members of the *Kalmia* genus, the leaves of mountain laurel contain a nerve toxin, andromedotoxin. This poison causes terrible salivation and paralysis in livestock, especially sheep, which seem drawn to the lush foliage. Amazingly, grouse and deer both browse its leaves and buds with no apparent ill effects.

Habitat: *Rocky, acidic woods*
Flowers: *June to early July*
Status: *Uncommon in southern and western areas*

Mountain Laurel *Kalmia latifolia*

HOBBLEBUSH
Viburnum lantanoides

The bane of cross-country hikers and trail crews on all New England mountainsides, this medium-size shrub has also been called witch-hobble, tangle-legs, and a number of more colorful names. Perhaps the most interesting name given to the plant is she-moosewood, bestowed by Maine lumberjacks in the mistaken belief that this was the female form of the striped maple. The maple, with its pointed but otherwise similar leaves, was called he-moosewood, or maleberry, an intriguing oxymoron. Both plants are well loved by the moose, a ruminating animal fond of the juicy leaves, bark, and twigs found on these unrelated species.

Hobblebush is distinctive throughout the year. Well described as a straggling shrub, the arching branches have the habit of reaching down to the ground. Here they often take root at the tips, forming nasty loops of limber wood that catch the feet of careless passersby. Ranked along these branches are large, heavy-veined, round leaves. When heavily browsed by moose or deer, the plant grows replacement leaves that are narrower, thinner, and more coarsely toothed than the originals.

This duality of form is also present in the flowers, appearing in clusters, like unmelted snowballs, in the cold spring woods. The outer flowers are about 1 inch across and, lacking sexual parts, purely for show—especially when they are pink, as in form *roseum*. The inner blossoms are small, individually inconspicuous, but all business, containing both stamens and pistils. Fertilized by early insects, these become clusters of bright red berries that ripen to black. The berries usually disappear into animal mouths before the season turns the leaves bronze-red.

Throughout the winter, hobblebush remains easy to identify because next year's leaves form in the fall. Lacking bud scales to shelter them, the tan incipient leaves are apparent at the ends of the arching branches, looking like tiny praying hands.

Sometimes called wayfaring tree for its resemblance to that European species (which lacks the two-flowered blossoms), hobblebush is a delightful trailside companion for those who stay on the paths of New England's mountains. Growing up to about 3,000 feet in elevation and flourishing in old second-growth forests, it is a reminder of the return of that lumbering ungulate that is so fond of moosewood browse.

Habitat: *Woods and ravines*
Flowers: *May to early June*
Status: *Fairly common throughout New England*

Hobblebush   *Viburnum lantanoides*

Stream, Green Mountains

Pond, Berkshire Mountains

STREAMBANKS
AND POND SHORES

Where water meets the land there exists a complex and fascinating net-work of plants, soil, and hydrology that renders benefits to wildlife and people alike. The free services that the borders of ponds, lakes, and rivers provide are innumerable. The ways in which these wetlands and their components interrelate and function is poorly understood; the ways in which they are impacted by thoughtless human activities is well documented, and blithely ignored.

By shading and cooling the water column and providing overhangs for breeding and resting areas, naturally vegetated riparian banks found along streams provide a refuge for freshwater fish such as brook and rainbow trout. Woody plants like speckled alder, pink azalea, red maple, eastern hemlock, northern white cedar, tamarack, and yellow birch anchor these banks and prevent erosion. The dense roots and rhizomes trap and filter sediment before it reaches the water. Overhanging branches provide perch-ing sites for fish-eating birds such as green herons, kingfishers, and osprey. Herbaceous wetland plants provide food and cover for a variety of aquatic and terrestrial insects, amphibians, waterfowl, and mammals.

Wetlands bordering ponds and streams also improve water quality by absorbing nutrients such as nitrogen and phosphorus contained in runoff from development and stormwater outfalls; these nutrients can cause eutrophication and anoxic conditions, especially in smaller water bodies. Plants and organic soils found along streams and pond shores act as "sinks" for a variety of toxic substances such as aluminum, boron, copper, zinc, and magnesium. Many wetland plants such as alder and sweet gale can actually fix atmospheric nitrogen, storing it in root nodules where it is eventually released into the soil.

The value of wetlands to wildlife is well documented. The interface between deep water (greater than 6 feet) and upland creates an ecotone or edge that provides close proximity to the amenities of both worlds. About two-thirds of the fish species harvested in the United States spawn in fresh-water wetlands. Rare and endangered animal species are disproportionately represented in wetland habitats: half of the amphibian and a third of the bird species listed under the federal Endangered Species Act are wetland dependent.

Plants that grow in saturated soils or in areas periodically inundated by flooding are stressed due to lack of oxygen or a shallow zone of aeration. Terrestrial plants usually respire through stomata located on the underside of their leaves. Shoreline species must use a variety of adaptations to obtain needed oxygen. These survival strategies include a shallow but broad root system growing above the anaerobic zone, or formation of lateral roots put out directly from trunk or branches. Willows, black spruce, northern white cedar, and alders form these adventitious roots in floodplain areas. It is often possible to gauge historic flood levels by observing the height of these roots on the trunks of wetland trees and shrubs.

Other herbaceous species such as bladderworts, water lilies, and marsh marigold take oxygen directly from water through the entire surface of the leaves and stem. Still other plants have an ingenious feedback shutdown system. When carbon dioxide, a by-product of respiration, begins to reach intolerable levels in the plants' tissues, a biochemical signal is generated, lowering the plants' oxygen needs until aerated conditions return. Oxygen deprivation is less a problem along fast-flowing rivers and streams where movement increases oxygenation.

The one value of a lakeshore or streamside that impresses on a more personal level is the serenity and beauty of the landscape. The arrival of spring is heralded by the golden visage of marsh marigold, eagerly sought by winter-weary New Englanders. The deep stillness of Vermont's Lake Willoughby has more than once acted as a balm for sore muscles and skinned shins after a day of ledge-hopping on the cliffs above. The hypnotic sound of rushing water from snowmelt in the White Mountains' Ammonoosuc River or the bracing freshness of a dip in Maine's Saco on a sultry summer's afternoon soothes the soul in these frantic times.

PINK AZALEA or ELECTION PINK
Rhododendron prinophyllum

With flaring corolla and arching stamens, the pink azalea bursts into startling flower from its anonymous presence in thickets and rocky wood edges throughout central and western New England. Its fragrant pink trumpets seem all the more dramatic due to its habit of blooming before its leaves fully expand in early to mid-May, exposing what one old botany text describes as "its naked umbels."

As in all azaleas, this species shows off a five-lobed corolla with long exserted stamens topped by an even longer pistil. A pollinator, most likely a bumblebee laden with pollen, must brush by the sticky stigma to get to the nectar deep in the flower. The result more often than not is cross-pollination.

In general, Latin or Greek scientific names are more useful than colloquial names to describe individual species. This is not the case with pink azalea, with no less than four scientific names attributed to two closely related "pink azaleas"; *Rhododendron roseum* (now *R. prinophyllum*) and *R. nudiflorum* (now *R. periclymenoides*). English names are as numerous: election pink, pinxter flower, early azalea, and wild honeysuckle.

Apparently the major difference between the two pink azaleas is fragrance; this species has a delicious sweet scent whereas the second is scentless. Both are commonly raided in the wild for gardens and landscaping.

Pink azalea belongs to a great and diverse genus within the heath family. Closely related plants include the rhododendrons (see the chapter "Forest Slopes") and laurels. A rule of thumb to tell them apart is that all azaleas are deciduous whereas mountain laurel, bog laurel, and the rhododendrons are evergreen. All three groups form the famed balds or slicks of the Appalachian Mountains' highest peaks in Virginia and North Carolina. They're also called hells for the formidable obstacle they present to foot travel.

Experienced hikers are familiar with mayapples or swamp apples formed in late spring by a fungus on wild azaleas. These galls are juicy and a refreshing repast for the thirsty walker. Mountain folk even pickle them for later use.

Habitat: *Rocky, acidic woods and shores*
Flowers: *May to June*
Status: *Uncommon except in southern half of area; not in Maine*

Pink Azalea or Election Pink *Rhododendron prinophyllum*

TALL MEADOW RUE
Thalictrum pubescens

Clusters of white, starburst flowers atop massed green foliage mark the meadow rue as one of the distinctive flowers of midsummer. An obligate wetland species, the rue grows only along streams and in damp meadows, though reaching as high as the alpine ravines of New England and as low as the Georgia mountains. Since the flowers have no petals they do not catch the eye individually, but create a gauzy backdrop to the streams they shadow.

The common name rue is from its resemblance to the garden rue, of the genus *Ruta* or "herb of grace," an aromatic plant with fernlike leaves. The origin of the scientific name *Thalictrum* is lost to botanical antiquity: the Greek herbalist Dioscorides used the name for "some plant." An alternate species name is *Thalictrum polygamum*, and there hangs a tale.

Lacking petals, the meadow rue flower may not demand attention, yet it is the key to the plant's evolution. By microscopic characters, meadow rue is related to the buttercups and their kin—anemones, marsh marigolds, and columbines. Most of these plants have regular flowers with many stamens and several unconnected carpels. This condition is considered primitive, denoting a family with a long and vibrant lineage.

The finely cut leaves (like columbine's), the broad green sepals, and the clear acrid juice of the stem also relate it to other buttercups. Most plants in the family are known for having separate male and female flowers. But, as the name *polygamum* indicates, meadow rue occasionally sports a *bisexual* flower—one on which female pistils dominate, but a few male stamens appear on the outside of the flower. Examining the flowers this closely in the field will have the added advantage of close-up views of the bees and butterflies that pollinate the blossoms.

Tall meadow rue is an apt name for plants that grow upward of 10 feet tall in the best locations. Yet there are fonder titles such as muskrat-weed (a kind of guilt-by-association name), king-of-the-meadow (presumptuous?), and feather columbine, a perfect comparative description for both the flower and the leaf.

Habitat: *Streambanks, wet meadows up to alpine areas*
Flowers: *July and August*
Status: *Common, within its wetland habitats*

Tall Meadow Rue   *Thalictrum pubescens*

MARSH MARIGOLD
Caltha palustris

Even as the last of the mountain snowmelt is freshening streams and rivulets in the wet meadows below, the bright gold of the "marsh goblet" enriches all who take the time to notice. This hardy herb of early spring can turn a muddy roadside ditch into a river of sunshine yellow, a botanic Midas touch if there ever was one.

Marsh marigold's sometimes spectacular displays and colonizing abilities give it the aspect of an alien species, yet it is native in all six New England states. Its succulent hollow stems and leaves form a green bower in contrast with the sunny five- to-nine-petaled flowers. The large blossoms look like robust buttercups—no mistake considering this species' place in the crowfoot or buttercup family.

The sprawling kidney-shaped leaves have been used as a potherb for generations and are considered an excellent source of vitamin A and riboflavin. Knowledgeable preparation, however, is critical because the uncooked leaves and buds contain poisonous alkaloids. These poisons are rendered harmless only with two changes of boiling water, a tedious process that should deter the inexperienced natural foods gatherer.

Some sources indicate that grazing stock have been poisoned and milk production tainted by the animals' nibbling on the inviting green shoots. One old botanical journal indicates that human consumption of raw herbage produced "intoxication" and erratic behavior.

Ojibwa Indians mixed a root tea made from this plant with maple sugar to concoct a fine cough syrup used commonly by white settlers in northern New England. The plant was also called capers for the pickled flower buds that taste similar to the modern condiment.

A plant's human history can often be measured by the number of colloquial names it has gathered. Marsh marigold must have a rich history. At one time or another it's been called cowslip, king-cup, palsy-wort, boots, crazy bet, gools, and drunkards (the last three undoubtedly by those foolish enough to eat the plant raw).

Habitat: *Wet meadows and slow streams*
Flowers: *April and May*
Status: *Common in wetland habitats*

Marsh Marigold   *Caltha palustris*

WATER MAT or WATER CARPET
Chrysosplenium americanum

One blistering hot June day, we trudged wearily up the Dry River Wilderness trail on the way to the Monroe Flats and Mt. Washington's summit. Blackflies slaked their thirst in the pools of sweat and blood that formed in the crevices of our necks and faces. Botany can be a brutal business.

In a moment our pain turned to joy as we came upon a bitingly cold waterfall, whose swirling eddies of meltwater mixed with cool spring seeps on either side of the basin. As we sat refreshed after a good shower, we noticed a bright green herb sprawling over the wet mud. A closer examination revealed the tiny flowers of the much-overlooked water mat. Thus was christened Chrysosplenium Falls.

Water mat is a succulent aquatic, which through convergent evolution looks similar to other fleshy water plants like watercress *(Nasturtium officinale)* and water starwort *(Callitriche* spp.). As in these two other aquatics, water mat requires the clean, unpolluted cold water commonly found in spring heads and groundwater seeps.

Its roundish leaves are obscurely scalloped and arranged opposite each other on a square stem. The minute flowers lack petals, having four or five greenish yellow calyx lobes. Indeed, the most conspicuous features of the flower are the ten bright orange anthers arranged in a circle around the style.

Although not thought of as a high-elevation species, water mat has been found in the damp peats of the Alpine Garden on Mt. Washington. This humble, yet interesting member of the saxifrage family deserves a better name, such as its less common handle, golden saxifrage.

Habitat: *Cold springs and mud*
Flowers: *Mid-May to late June*
Status: *Fairly common*

Water Mat or Water Carpet
Chrysosplenium americanum

WATER AVENS or PURPLE AVENS
Geum rivale

Water avens is a curious plant found commonly in wet meadows and bogs throughout northern New England. Rising from a basal whorl of compound leaves, the drooping globose flowers hang singly from a long leafless peduncle, bobbing eerily about like disembodied eyeballs. The pink veins of the yellow petals give these eyeballs a distinctly bloodshot look.

Flowering throughout the summer, water avens is usually found at lower elevations but will also grow on the wet headwalls of some alpine ravines at 4,000 to 5,000 feet.

Most species of the *Geum* genus have been known since antiquity for their flavorful roots and rhizomes; *geum* is Greek for "to taste well." Being representative of this tasty genus, water avens is also known as Indian chocolate or chocolate root for its qualities as a natural hot cocoa. Its long taproot can be boiled to produce a chocolaty beverage, though our sources tell us to bring plenty of milk and sweetener to cut a rather pungent aftertaste. This may explain its other widespread historic use as an astringent.

Habitat: *Wet meadows, roadside ditches*
Flowers: *May to June*
Status: *Uncommon*

Water Avens or Purple Avens   *Geum rivale*

CANADA LILY
Lilium canadense

In early July as the New England summer begins to really simmer, one of nature's richest displays can be witnessed in wet meadows and fields throughout the region. The wild yellow (a.k.a. Canada) lily rises handsomely to a height of 6 feet from a 1½-inch-wide perennial bulb. The long, glaucous stem is marked by 6 to 11 whorls of lance-shaped leaves arranged in a circular fashion around it. Atop this impressive stalk is an inflorescence of up to two dozen blossoms hanging pendulously with wide-starting stamens and pistil.

The nodding flowers themselves can be yellow, orange, or orange-red, with black mottling within the perianth. Like most members of Liliaceae, the flower parts are in multiples of three; three petals and three sepals alternate around six arching stamens, with a three-parted stigma topping the long pistil. The sepals and petals are identical, making them tepals in some botanists' eyes. The tepals are only slightly curled back at the tips, unlike the sharply reflexed ones found on the somewhat similar Turk's-cap lily.

All 6 feet of herbaceous biomass emerges annually from a small scaly bulb used for centuries by American Indians for both food and medicine. A natural mucilage found in the bulb was used to thicken soups and stews. Colonists picked up on this natural okra substitute, as well as its reputed value as a digestive restorative in root-tea form. Although harvesting took a toll, yellow lily numbers today are relatively healthy, with this species still being the commonest wild lily in New England.

Canada lily ranges from Nova Scotia south through western New England to the high mountains of Virginia and North Carolina, where it grows to 6,000 feet in elevation. A plant of uplands and mountains in the southern United States, this lily is most often seen in wet meadows and seasonally wet roadside ditches near the lower slopes in New England. Unlike our yellow to orange flower, the southern variety commonly is a deep blood red.

Habitat: *Wet meadows, roadside ditches*
Flowers: *July to early August*
Status: *Fairly common*

Canada Lily   *Lilium canadense*

GREAT ANGELICA
Angelica atropurpurea

When encountered in the rich, streambank soils of Vermont's Northeast Kingdom or the rugged country of northern New Hampshire, this plant seems oddly robust—almost tropical in the prodigious amount of biomass it produces each year. And all of this plant from a seed not much bigger than a caraway seed (which grows on a related member of the carrot family).

Angelica gets its name from the reputation of some members of the genus to produce an "angelic" cordial or tonic. This species reputedly can be eaten if cooked in a double boiler, tasting like stewed celery. (Is the world ready for a substitute for stewed celery?) Caution must remain the watch-word for would-be tasters of any wild members of this family; the other, similar, New England species is *Angelica venenosa* (*venenosa* means "very poisonous"). *Never eat any wild plant from this family.*

The tall size and dark purple stem of roadside plants are a cue to identification of great angelica, even at highway speeds. The plant, with a geographical range that stretches from Labrador to Iowa, also grows in a wide range of elevations, from lowland valleys to headwalls of alpine ravines in the Presidential Range. In both of these locations look for the other large umbellifer (carrot family member), cow parsnip, with more noticeable white flowers than this greenish species.

Both plants have stout stems with swollen petioles beneath the ternately compound (divided and roughly triangular) leaves. The cow parsnip is far leafier than the angelica, but both hold a celery connection in this regard as well, for if you look at a clump of celery in your refrigerator you will see the swollen petiole base and compound leaf characteristic of this family.

Related species grow high in the Rocky Mountains and on the long, solitary ranges of New Zealand—botanical threads linking New England's mountains to a wider world.

Habitat: *Streambanks, hill country and alpine*
Flowers: *June to September (green fruits are more conspicuous than flowers)*
Status: *Uncommon in most locales*

Great Angelica   *Angelica atropurpurea*

TALL CONEFLOWER
Rudbeckia laciniata

The bewildering variety of flowers in the composite family—more than 20,000 species identified worldwide—is the mark of a group of plants that has arrived rather recently in the earth's history. As evolution rapidly unfolds, the composites exhibit subtle differences from species to species, from genera to genera, challenging taxonomist and amateur enthusiast alike. In western America tall coneflower is one of the so-called DYCs—the "damned yellow composites," including scores of similar sunflower-like blossoms.

Also known as cut-leaf coneflower or green-headed coneflower, all the common names are really just descriptions of the flower's appearance. As a group, coneflowers are named for the tightly packed cluster of disk florets at the center of the flower head. In *Rudbeckia hirta*, the black-eyed Susan, this is a brown to black button. In this species it is a green inverted cone, protruding from the swept-back, lemon yellow ray flowers. The flowers cluster distinctively above the deeply cut (laciniate) leaves atop stalks that can top 12 feet in height.

Native Americans, with their dependence on a natural pharmacopeia, were able to distinguish coneflower from other yellow composites with studied ease. Though the plant is somewhat poisonous to livestock, it could still be used medicinally. A hot bath with a bushel of coneflower plants mixed in was used as a relief of rheumatic pains or as an antidote for the bites of snakes and insects. The yellow liquid extracted by boiling the flowers was applied to poison ivy rash with effective results. Such uses were probably as widespread as the plant itself, which can be found north into Quebec, south to Florida, and west to Arizona and Montana.

In New England tall coneflower is almost always found in wet meadows and ditches. Rarely encountered in the granite country to the east, this flower is typical of Vermont's gulfs and ravine streambanks, much as it can be found along Rocky Mountain creeks. A variety of the flower (var. *hortense*) in which the ray flowers are doubled is called golden glow. This flashy, chrysanthemum-like bloom on tall stalks is a mainstay of up-country gardens and occasionally wanders into the wild to bloom alongside its wild kin.

Habitat: *Wet meadows, streambanks, ditches*
Flowers: *August and September*
Status (typical form): *Rare in Maine and New Hampshire, fairly common in Vermont and Berkshires*
Status (golden glow): *Uncommon garden escape naturalized to roadsides and old fields*

Tall Coneflower *Rudbeckia laciniata*

INDIAN POKE
Veratrum viride

The virulence of the poison derived from the fibrous roots of Indian poke has led to a number of stories. Certainly the one that most strains credibility is the one that tells how Native Americans selected their chiefs by treating candidates to a serving of this plant. Those who lived were chosen. Though probably apocryphal, the story offers us an interesting alternative to the expensive hype of the modern American political process.

All seven native North American species of *Veratrum* contain a poison called veratrin. Properly processed, this poison has proven to be the source of a valuable drug used in the treatment of high blood pressure. To animals the ingestion of the plant is less useful; a powerful and violent narcotic, it is often fatal. Even when taken in nonlethal doses, veratrin is known to cause birth defects when eaten by pregnant sheep, producing lambs with deformed heads. Even the flowers are said to be poisonous to insects and may result in the death of honeybees. The Quebecois may have the best name for the plant—*tabac de Diable*, "devil's tobacco." Still another name, itchweed, recognizes one of the afflictions it causes.

Throughout rural northern New England the plant appears early in the season, poking up odd green spears in wetlands from river bottoms to well above tree line. Reminiscent of and often called skunk cabbage, Indian poke slowly unfurls immense pleated leaves with the typical parallel veination of the lily family. Rising on a stout, hairy stalk, the leaves can rise to 4 feet in height. But they signify little, fading, insect eaten (by borers immune to veratrin) and blackened by the time the pyramidal cluster of green flowers appears in midsummer—if indeed the flowers appear on the stalk at all.

On close examination the flowers are surprisingly charming, each a perfect miniature lily with three green sepals and (an oddity among flowers) three green petals. This six-part flower is flecked with spots of yellow from its six stamens. Often called false hellebore, from some fancied resemblance to the European garden plant *Helleborus*, the Indian poke is a welcome green harbinger in otherwise sere and muddy ditches or along bare alpine rills in advancing spring.

Habitat: *Wet meadows, streambanks, swamps*
Flowers: *June and July*
Status: *Common in most damp mountain habitats*

Indian Poke   *Veratrum viride*

PURPLE-STEMMED ASTER
Aster puniceus

Asters are among the world's best-loved flowers, growing as easily in gardens as in field, forest, meadow, or wetland. Also called frost flower, for their appearance late in the year, and starwort for their starburst shape, they are mostly two-toned composites with yellow central disks and vari-colored rays.

Aster puniceus is, by its species name, designated as the "red or purple" one, a reference not to the flower but to the color of the stout stem with its harsh white hairs and rough, clasping leaves. Growing exclusively in wet areas, purple-stemmed aster expresses fall through much of the moist, mountainous country of New England. The flowers, pale lavender with dull yellow centers, share the composites' evolutionary device of making many small flowers look like a single large one. Insects stumble across scores of blossoms, pollinating many from pollen gathered on their visit to another plant.

So successful is this strategy that asters are evolving and changing even as we study them, leading to a confusion of forms. We see the result of these rapid changes in some of the varieties or forms of this flower that botanists have recognized. Variety *oligocephalus* ("few-headed"), for example, inhabits our subalpine ravines, as well as other frigid places such as Labrador, Newfoundland, and Saskatchewan. Forms *albiflorus* ("white-flowered") and *demissus* are occasionally found in Coos County, New Hampshire, whereas a variety with a smooth stem (var. *firmus*) frequently grows in Maine's Acadia National Park.

Oddly, what may seem at first glance to be simply an exercise in botanical trivia, is in fact a lesson in evolutionary biology. The various forms of purple-stemmed aster are a record of its participation in life's most vital activity, the exploration of the diversity of forms to fit a variety of environments.

Habitat: *Wet areas: meadows, streambanks, swamps, woods*
Flowers: *August and September*
Status: *Typical form very common; var.* oligocephalus *local in the White Mountains*

Purple-Stemmed Aster   *Aster puniceus*

TURTLEHEAD
Chelone glabra

A rewarding adventure for bees is the forced crawl through the throat of a turtlehead flower. Like many plants in the figwort family, turtlehead has fused petals that form a deep, tubular flower. The hoodlike upper lobe and concave lower lip give the blossom an oddly reptilian mein—all in the name of ensuring cross-pollination by bees.

Look closely at the nearly closed mouth of this "turtle" and you'll notice a lure for the bees: a tuft of yellow hairs on the lower petal just inside the throat, advertising the nectar and pollen found inside. There, too, you'll see a long protruding style, a snakelike tongue that accounts for the less common name of snakehead. When the bee forces its way into the flower in search of food, pollen from other flowers is deposited at the end of this style, which is simply a tube down which the pollen can grow to deliver sperm to the waiting eggs. One enjoyable, if vaguely violent, sport is to remove the fading flower heads (fresh ones will not come off easily), leaving behind the long tongue of the style and the developing seed capsule below.

Everything about turtlehead is singular in appearance. Paired, lance-shape leaves with sharp-toothed edges are often covered with a whitish mildew by flowering time. The stout stem is square in cross section, the flowers unmistakable, and these give way to knobbly clusters of fruit caps. Combine with the wetland habitat and you have a plant that almost speaks its own name, *Chelone*, Greek for "a tortoise."

Like many other members of its family, including foxglove, snapdragon, and penstemon, turtlehead can be grown in gardens. Horticulturists usually prefer dark pink species like *Chelone lyonii*, and these flowers grow in apparently wild stations where escaped from cultivation. Worth searching out is *C. glabra* variety *elatior*, with purple at the base and lip of the flower. This variety is reported from several locations in our area including Wilmington, Vermont, and Jaffrey and Lincoln, New Hampshire.

Habitat: *Streams and wetlands*
Flowers: *August and September*
Status: *White variety common; var.* elatior *rare*

Turtlehead   *Chelone glabra*

SPOTTED JOE-PYE WEED
Eupatorium maculatum

In late summer wet meadows and low fields throughout New England become a sea of purple, colored by the large floral heads of spotted joe-pye weed. This stately perennial stands as tall as 10 feet high, an impressive expenditure of energy for an herbaceous plant that dies back to ground level every year.

There are several species of joe-pye weed within the vast genus *Eupatorium*. This northern species is typified by a flat-topped corymb of 8 to 20 florets with a solid pith and purple-streaked stem. Other closely related species by the same name have rounded "domes" of flowers, hollow piths, and glaucous stems. All have coarsely toothed, lanceolate leaves in whorls of four to five around the stem.

Spotted joe-pye weed has a long history of Native American and European colonial use as an herbal remedy for fever and ague. Linnaeus named the genus after the legendary Mithridates Eupator, a first century B.C. Mesopotamian physician who used an infusion of the leaves and flowers as a fever reducer.

Contrary to popular belief, Joe Pye was not an Indian medicine man or shaman but a nineteenth-century Caucasian who traveled the western United States as an Indian theme promoter, a kind of Elmer Gantry snake oil merchant who espoused the merits of the plant's roots as a sweat inducer to combat the effects of typhus fever.

Ranging from the lowlands of Quebec and Nova Scotia to the uplands and mountains of Tennessee and North Carolina, joe-pye weed has also been called thoroughwort, boneset, motherwort, kidneyroot, and king of the meadow.

Habitat: *Wet meadows and streambanks*
Flowers: *August to October*
Status: *Common*

Spotted Joe-Pye Weed   *Eupatorium maculatum*

Quaking sphagnum bog, central New Hampshire

BOGS AND FENS

New England peatlands, pockets of waterlogged soil consisting of a thick accumulation of dead vegetation, beckon to the naturalist with the lure of rare or unusual plants and a taste of the boreal landscape. Bogs and fens defy the familiarity of the surrounding forests and human developments. A favorite example is the Philbrick-Cricenti bog in New London, New Hampshire, where, while listening to the background roar of motorized civilization, you can gaze across an open mat of vegetation to a fringe of tamarack and black spruce. The scene more than imitates the arctic muskeg; the very same tree species venture the farthest north of any on the continent. Remnants of the reign of Boreas—god of the arctic wind—New England's bogs are rich with the untamed spirit of the far north.

The idealized bog, whether a tiny mountain wetland or a sprawling lowland basin, creates a characteristic vegetative pattern. Mapped by plant type or viewed from the air, this classic pattern consists of concentric rings of plants: first the circle of hardy conifers, then a broad sweep of heath shrubs, giving way to a low carpet of moss, sedge, and herbs, ending at a central "eye" of dark water rich in organic acids. This ideal is seldom realized, each bog revealing a specific character dependent on the forces that formed and sustain it.

Scientists are still exploring bog dynamics. Conventional wisdom considered all bogs to be glacial artifacts, ice-edge ponds filling in to become dry land, with the bog an intriguing intermediate stage. Long-term studies now question the universal applicability of this model. Many large bogs defy the conventional pattern of in-fill, appearing to be self-perpetuating. The vast raised bogs of Maine grow above the surrounding terrain, and scientists believe many are spreading rather than shrinking. All indications are that bogs are a constant in the New England landscape.

The term bog, widely used to describe any wetland, is best reserved for those areas contained in a closed basin and dominated by sphagnum moss. Sphagnum's ability to grow upon itself, forming deep, saturated beds of earlier mossy generations, results in the quaking bog, which can be so much fun or so treacherous to walk across. Sphagnum mats do float, and it is possible for the walker to break through into deep, cold water for an unexpected bath—or worse. Bog water is highly acidic due to the tannic acid slowly released by vegetation steeped there. The chemical character of sphagnum adds to the acidity. The moss readily exchanges hydrogen ions from its cells to adsorb minerals: the H^+ increases the acidity of the water by degrees.

Acidity precludes the growth of bacteria and makes for a sterile aquatic environment poor in the stuff of life. Animal and human bodies extracted from bogs are found in marvelous states of preservation. These bog mummies are the natural result of waters in which lack of oxygen and bacteria nullifies decomposition. In such conditions, the slow recycling of nutrients from dead vegetation leads to a dominance of plants with special adaptations to life in nutrient-poor environments. The heaths, like rhodora, use nitrogen in an ionic form more readily available than that used by most plants. All orchids are notoriously difficult to transplant due to their symbiotic relationship with soil fungi that provide nutrients to the plants. Most intriguing to humans are the so-called carnivorous plants, which capture, digest, and absorb nutrients from insects. Cold is another characteristic of bogs, and plants adapted to low temperatures thrive there. Tamarack trees in Siberia are known to survive temperatures of 85 degrees below zero!

Bogs get their water supply from rain and snow—new nutrients are scarce. Richer peatlands, supplied with minerals by surface or groundwater flow, are called fens. The availability of nutrients makes for a very different plant community in fens, often dominated by grasslike sedges rather than sphagnum moss. The *flow* of water is vital to fens, so they are often located on slopes rather than in depressions. Rich fens, where waters containing calcium (lime) neutralize acid and favor the growth of sedge meadows, are naturalists' favorites, particularly when seeking spectacular species such as the showy lady's-slipper. Abundant only in areas of limestone bedrock, rich fens are most common in Vermont. Poor fens, on the other hand, are a common wetland type—the most famous being the fens that were filled in to create the land that is now Fenway Park.

In southern New England, bogs and fens have been brutally converted to other uses. Naturally uncommon, these special wetland communities were far too easy to fill in as development spread across the adjacent uplands and forests. Seen as breeders of mosquitoes and "bad air," bogs and fens suffered for the sake of human comfort. Awareness of the value of wetlands is widespread today; all states and the federal government have protective laws of varying degrees of effectiveness. Perhaps this is enough. But some of us see bogs and fens as the last refuges of an array of plants and animals that can enrich the lives of those who, with uncertain tread and damp feet, seek out these ancient and secret haunts.

BOG LAUREL or PALE LAUREL
Kalmia polifolia

Near the top of the Tuckerman Ravine headwall, within a wet snowball's throw of the most popular trail to the top of Mt. Washington, a large patch of pink-flowered bog laurel adds color to the alpine spring. Snowmelt and mountain fogs make this otherwise rocky perch a fine location for this denizen of northern bogs.

Although superficially similar to the more common sheep laurel, which is much more catholic in its choice of habitats, bog laurel is easily distinguished in detail. The flowers, with the hair-trigger stamens common to all laurels, are a paler pink than those of sheep laurel. This white complexion is evident on the undersides of the leaves as well. Closer inspection of the leaves reveals in-rolled edges, a cold-weather adaptation shared with other members of the heath family. Arrangement of leaves and flowers is an important identification feature: leaves on bog laurel occur in opposite pairs and the flowers bloom at the end of the woody stems.

All laurels have a chemical defense system that deters browsing, widely noted by sheep that have the misfortune of eating the leaves or twigs. The toxin that is responsible for "lamb-kill" is called acetylandromedol or andromedatoxin, a name derived from the related bog heath, *Andromeda*. Though you are not likely to browse a laurel plant, the poison is in all the plant parts and some scientists suggest that bee's honey made from laurel blooms may be toxic.

Another biochemical advantage of the heath family helps bog laurel grow in the acid-rich, nutrient-poor standing waters of a bog. In a place where some plants have been moved to carnivorous ways to supply vital nitrogen compounds, the bog laurel derives nitrogen from the ammonium ion, a form more plentiful than the nitrate form used by most plants. Fungus-root relationships, tough leaves, and cell chemicals that deter infection are all a part of the scarcely visible lifestyle that brings pale laurel blossoms to a mountain bog.

Habitat: *Bogs, moist alpine areas*
Flowers: *Mid-May to June*
Status: *Common, within its restricted habitat*

Bog Laurel or Pale Laurel   *Kalmia polifolia*

LEATHERLEAF or CASSANDRA
Chamaedaphne calyculata

One of the most important bog builders in the Northern Hemisphere, the low evergreen shrub leatherleaf often forms acres of impenetrable tangles. A prolific colonizer, leatherleaf, along with sphagnum moss, can create a floating mat over small ponds, resulting in a most unique natural trampoline known as a quaking bog. Commonly leatherleaf grows in damp acidic peatlands or on pond shores in full sunlight.

Leatherleaf lives up to its name with alternate, tough leathery leaves that hang on for a year until new leaves are nearly formed. With the one year lifespan, leatherleaf is more accurately described as semievergreen. This adaptation allows continuous photosynthesis and nutrient conservation. The leaves are dull green above and a rusty brown beneath.

One of the earliest of the north country's shrubs to bloom, the one-sided, leafy racemes begin to blossom in mid-April. The small white flowers are typically urn shaped, as are many other members of the Ericaceae or heath family.

While some herbals suggest a tea infused from the leaves to ward off infections and inflammations, the leaves contain the poisonous substance andromedatoxin, making them unpalatable not only to large herbivores but also to fungus diseases, bacteria, and viruses. This is contradicted by at least one source, which describes it as a favorite browse for hares and cottontails.

Occurring in all circumpolar regions of the world, leatherleaf ranges from Canada south to the mountains of Georgia. In northern New England it comes in two varieties: *angustifolia*, with leaves one-third as wide as long and growing in lowland bogs; and *latifolia*, with much wider leaves, sometimes found growing near tree line on our highest peaks.

In autumn, leatherleaf turns a handsome bronze, lending a warm hue to the golds and scarlets of New England's foliage season.

Habitat: *Acidic bogs*
Flowers: *April to May*
Status: *Common*

Leatherleaf or Cassandra   *Chamaedaphne calyculata*

SHOWY LADY'S-SLIPPER
Cypripedium reginae

Enthusiasm for this largest of the wild New England orchids pervades the otherwise technical descriptions of taxonomic botanists. Anyone who has had the privilege of seeing the pink-and-white blossoms in one of their secretive, swampy settings would probably agree that the flower is spectacular. *Spectabile* (Latin for "showy") is another name once given to the plant, although *Cypripedium reginae* ("of the queen") is today's accepted species name.

The popularity of orchids from an aesthetic viewpoint was noted in ancient Oriental and Greek texts. Their coveted beauty is partly responsible for their rarity. Although the stem and leaves are covered with a dense armor of irritating hairs, which can cause a serious skin inflammation much like poison ivy, the temptation to gather for the table arrangement or to transplant to a more accessible site is strong (particularly if a profit can be made). Add to this pressure the destruction of the calcareous swamp and fen habitat of showy lady's-slipper and the result is a plant legally classified as endangered in two New England states and of special concern in two others.

Scientific interest in orchids has always been high. Much early research focused on the unique pollination mechanisms, so important to provide seed for the greenhouse and garden. Germination of collected seed in gardens proved to be even more difficult than producing seed. Microscopic investigations revealed the reasons. Unlike other plants, orchids produce tiny seeds lacking a food source for the incipient plant. Instead, provided that they fall into the proper soil medium, the seeds form a small corm that waits in dormancy until invaded by a symbiotic fungus. Attracted to and feeding on a portion of the seed, the fungus provides the embryonic plant with vital nutrients to begin growth.

Nature ultimately provides the necessary time for seed to link with fungus and grow to maturity. Humans may save the necessary habitats for this small miracle to take place. No one expects the queen's slipper to be common, but all should respect the corners of the castle where it lives.

Habitat: *Fens, swamps, in limy areas*
Flowers: *Mid-June to July*
Status: *Rare; endangered in New Hampshire and Connecticut*

Showy Lady's-Slipper   *Cypripedium reginae*

BOG ROSEMARY OR PALE ANDROMEDA
Andromeda polifolia var. *glaucophylla*

Carolus Linnaeus named this low, evergreen heath after Andromeda, the fair maiden of Greek mythology who was tied to a rock to await the ravishment of the sea monster Cetus. Fortunately for Andromeda, the hero Perseus was riding by on his flying horse and saved her for scientific posterity, providing a name for an overlooked peatland plant, as well as a neighboring galaxy. The English alias rosemary refers not to a fair maiden but to the garden spice, which this plant resembles.

Native Americans were said to have made a tea from the plant, but modern herbalists should be cautioned: the plant contains a potent poison called andromedatoxin. Evolved as a chemical defense against animal grazing, this substance is known to cause drastic reduction in blood pressure, breathing difficulty, vomiting, cramps, and diarrhea. Better to spend one's energies on searching out and admiring the plant.

Nowhere a major component of our mountain peatlands, bog rosemary grows throughout the region, usually in mineral-rich wetlands, making it a good indicator plant of fens. One colony is located in a ravine high on the alpine slopes of Mt. Katahdin.

Growing to perhaps 2 feet high, bog rosemary is best identified by its blue-green leaves (the meaning of its name *glaucophylla*), which stand out from the surrounding vegetation. Narrow, tough, and evergreen, the leaves have the in-rolled edges and underside hairs typical of plants living in cold bogs (see "Labrador Tea," page 88). Though slightly similar to pale laurel, *Andromeda* has far narrower leaves arranged alternately on the sparse branches. Flowers are pale, drooping bells and scarcely showy; the turban-shaped fruit capsules that follow are more distinctive, with their chestnut color and furrowed surface.

Andromeda can be grown in moist, peaty soils in the garden where its year-round foliage adds another tint to the gardener's palette. No need to dig up the whole plant: cuttings will grow well, or seed may be gathered sparingly. As for the flowers, Thoreau suggests: "A timid botanist would never pluck it."

Habitat: *Peatlands: fens, bogs, pond margins*
Flowers: *Late May to June*
Status: *Uncommon*

Bog Rosemary or Pale Andromeda   *Andromeda polifolia* var. *glaucophylla*

LABRADOR TEA
Ledum groenlandicum

Just who was it that first drank Labrador tea? Someone with a strong stomach, we suspect. In brewing Labrador tea the specific toxin ledol, a diuretic agent, is steeped from the leathery leaves. Depending on the source, this produces either a pleasant or potent tea or a drink of poor quality. Trappers, backwoodsmen, colonists, Indians, and Canadian travelers are all reputed to have made use of this boreal plant, also known as bog tea or Hudson's Bay tea. So far as we know, Celestial Seasonings has yet to file a trademark for *Ledum* tea.

An indicator plant of cold, northern bogs, Labrador tea also produces impressive displays when in bloom on alpine lawns. The flower clusters, each blossom five petaled with up to seven prominent stamens, have a showy quality that betrays their relation to rhododendrons. The evergreen leaves are lightly fragrant when crushed; the Latin name derives from the Greek for a similarly aromatic plant of the rockrose family.

Far more distinctive than the fragrance is the singular appearance of the leaves. Dark, leathery smooth on the upper surface, each leaf has rolled-down margins. Turn the leaf over and you'll see the distinctive rust-colored tomentum, or plant hairs, looking like a coat of orange felt. These leaf features are adaptations to the cold weather of the north country.

Scientists once believed that in-rolled margins, leathery tissue, hairiness, along with the waxy coverings and needle shapes seen in leaves of alpine plants, were primarily water conservation measures. Why conserve water in a bog? you ask. Good question: the original idea that acidity made bog water unavailable to plants has been dismissed. Scientists now know that for Labrador tea, cold's the thing.

Evergreen leaves, found in most bog heaths of our mountains, seem to give plants a competitive advantage at the margins of the growing season—late fall, early spring—when the leaf avails itself of the energy-giving photosynthetic process. This advantage has its disadvantage: the leaf must endure winter's cold. The rusty wool of Labrador tea leaves has an insulative power that seems to give it the competitive edge for survival in a boreal climate.

Habitat: *Peat soils: bogs and alpine areas*
Flowers: *Late May to July*
Status: *Common, within a restricted habitat*

Labrador Tea *Ledum groenlandicum*

SWEET FLAG
Acorus americanus

Sweet flag is a natural confection that grows in marshes throughout New England. Also known as sweet cane, sweet rush, and sweet sedge, it was used as a candy for generations in America, Europe, and Asia. Sweet flag is nonetheless potentially dangerous because of its close resemblance to other poisonous species. Without its characteristic golden spadix jutting out at an angle from the reedlike spathe, sweet flag's sword-shaped leaves and marsh habitat are a virtual match for the acrid blue flag (*Iris* spp.). Children have been poisoned in the past by mistaking blue flag root for the aromatic, pungent cinnamon-flavored rhizome of sweet flag.

The sectioned, unpeeled root was also used as a pharmaceutical into the early years of this century. Prescribed as calamus in the apothecary shop, the dried root was chewed as a palliative for digestive upsets and intestinal spasms.

There is plenty of scientific evidence that the compounds found in sweet flag root actually are better antispasmodics than the usually prescribed antihistamines. It was sold in the unpeeled state for three to six cents a pound in 1912. American Indians taught the colonists its usefulness in aiding a wide variety of digestive complaints. So popular did it become that it was introduced into England and continental Europe in the eighteenth century. There it still flourishes but rarely flowers.

An old recipe calls for the sectioning and peeling of the thick root into half-inch segments, boiling in four to five changes of water, then drying the pieces in brown sugar syrup. But to paraphrase an old mushroom-hunter's warning, "there are old sweet flag hunters and bold sweet flag hunters, but there are no old, bold sweet flag hunters."

Habitat: *Marshes, calm water*
Flowers: *June to July*
Status: *Uncommon*

Sweet Flag   *Acorus americanus*

PITCHER PLANT
Sarracenia purpurea

Romanticized as carnivorous plants, the several unrelated groups of wildflowers that trap insects are simply taking advantage of a source of nutrients otherwise scarce in their wetland environments. The pitcher plants—also known as sidesaddle flowers (a reference lost on we who live in a nonequine age) or huntsman's cups—are the most conspicuous of our plants that supplement their nutrient needs with protein drawn from captured insects.

The flower of the pitcher plant is a curious affair, reminiscent of the aliens who rose from the spacecraft in H. G. Wells's *War of the Worlds*. Like other intricate flowers, these are specially evolved to direct insects to the sexual organs. Openings between the royal purple petals and the umbrella-shaped style create a tunnel, effectively steering bees toward the pollen-bearing stamens and the pollen-receptive stigmas. Pendulous and bizarre, the flower's basic shape persists into winter as a fruit capsule standing high above the rosette of leaves at the base of the plant.

Pioneer botanist Linnaeus guessed that the pitcher-shaped leaf held reserve water in case of drought, an unlikely need in a bog. Today we understand the leaf's function in gathering, drowning, and digesting insects. Five distinct areas on the pitcher-shaped leaf provide the mechanics of its "carnivorous" ways. At the top is the attractant: a green hood with inviting red lines and sweet nectar, along with tricky downward-pointing hairs that keep the insect moving in the right direction. Below this is a slippery slide where plant cells adhere to the insect's six feet, but slide past each other (like tiles or playing cards), resulting in a plunge into the water collected in the leaf. Submerged areas of the leaf complete the process by secreting digestive enzymes (bacteria assist this process), holding the insects while the soft parts are dissolved and absorbed, and accumulating hard parts and directing nutrients to roots and flower stalks.

Despite the pitcher plant's inimical relationship with most insects, some opportunists take advantage of the leaf. Small frogs sometimes hunt on the lip of the leaf (careful not to fall in, as even they can be dissolved). There is even a type of moth that breeds exclusively in pitcher plants, using the leaf as a handy, weatherproof cocoon.

Habitat: *Sphagnum bogs*
Flowers: *Mid-June to July*
Status: *Fairly common throughout, in restricted habitat*

Pitcher Plant *Sarracenia purpurea*

RHODORA
Rhododendron canadense

Walk the Philbrick-Cricenti quaking bog trail in central New Hampshire on a fine day in late May and prepare to be overwhelmed with magenta clouds of rhodora mixed with the light pink of bog laurel and bog rosemary. This mass of color almost floats above the sphagnum mat, contrasted nicely against the mottled green backdrop of larch and black spruce. Throw the bizarre pitcher plant into this boreal mosaic and the otherworldly feel of a north country quaking bog is complete.

Rhodora is one of the few deciduous members of the Heath family. Before its leaves expand, the two-lipped flower bursts into bloom from mid-May in southern sections to late June in the far northern reaches of New England and Canada. Forming dense thickets with leatherleaf and other bog inhabitants, rhodora grows in good numbers in the low-lying lagg of peat bogs and occasionally on rocky subalpine ledges and cliffs. It ranges from Canada south to northern New Jersey and eastern Pennsylvania.

The individual flowers have a spidery look, with the three-lobed upper lip reaching over the two strap-shaped lower petals. The ten long stamens so characteristic of the azalea group are matched and even exceeded by the arching style and stigma. The flowers are closely arranged on a terminal umbel.

The interdependency of all species, faunal and floral, is most evident in these northern bogs where comparatively few species can thrive in the acidic, nutrient-poor conditions. One example is a rare butterfly, the bog elfin. The caterpillar of this insect has adapted to eat only the young leaves of the black spruce. A nearby rhodora may then quench the thirst of the adult butterfly.

Habitat: *Acidic bogs; rocky, peaty ledges*
Flowers: *May to June*
Status: *Fairly common*

Rhodora   *Rhododendron canadense*

WILD CALLA
Calla palustris

Groping unsteadily through a cold-water, black spruce bog near Stratton Mountain in Vermont one bright June morning, we were greeted by a veritable armada of the porcelain white spathes of wild calla. The contrast between the clean brilliance of the calla against the murky darkness of the water and peat of the bog is at once startling and cheering; how encouraging that from the swampy mire springs such purity of color.

Within the white flag of the spathe is the clublike spadix, as is typical in the Araceae (arum) family. The tiny flowers are arranged along this spadix, with male and female florets located on the lowest rung of the club ladder and males dominating the upper position (no socioeconomic statement is implied here).

Native Americans and other native peoples living within wild calla's circumpolar range have long used this species as a wild food. Linnaeus wrote how Laplanders made a wholesome bread from the ground rootstocks. Native Americans also made a nutritious but somewhat unpalatable flour by drying and grinding the root and seeds. This practice is best left to the experts; like all members of the arum family, most parts of the wild calla (but particularly the roots) contain the burning crystals of calcium oxalate. Indians used a tea distilled from its orbicular-cordate leaves to combat flu and snakebites.

Wild calla is most at home in boreal coniferous swamps and semiopen bogs, generally where water is at the surface much of the year. It is the only member of its family that makes a home in the cold northern regions of the world.

Flowering in June and July, the snowy spathes turn in late August to a bright cluster of crimson berries. Thus, in all seasons, wild calla, sometimes affectionately called the swamp robin, is a handsome and valuable component of northern wetlands.

Habitat: *Coniferous bogs and swamps*
Flowers: *June to July*
Status: *Uncommon*

Wild Calla *Calla palustris*

ROUND-LEAVED SUNDEW
Drosera rotundifolia

It comes as a surprise to many that the diminutive and often overlooked sundew, a glutinous carnivorous plant of bogs and wet ravines, riveted the attention of none other than Charles Darwin. In the later years of his life, Darwin devoted many experiments to the behavioral traits shared by plants and animals. During the 1870s Darwin demonstrated that sundews actually digest insects, that plant movement was instigated by the prey's struggling, and that sundews are omnivorous, digesting pollen, spores, and even leaves and seeds.

Each sundew leaf bristles with hundreds of ruby red glandular hairs, each tipped with a sticky secretion that entraps a wide range of hapless victims by acting as a kind of flypaper. From the tiniest gnat or mosquito to large dragonflies and monarch butterflies, digestion of the soft body parts within the hard exoskeleton begins immediately upon capture. The writing of the panicked insect stimulates other digesting glands to arch toward the locus of movement, further entrapping the guileless tidbit and eventually clogging its breathing apparatus, smothering lunch, so to speak. This dietary supplement, along with the more standard photosynthesis, offers a nutrient boost to a plant that usually grows in nutrient-poor acidic bogs.

The sundew, or *Drosera* (from the Greek *droseros* or "dewy") is sensitive to sunlight, refusing to open its flowers in anything but direct, midday sun. The flowers, arranged along a one-sided coil or scorpioid raceme, begrudgingly open one at a time—that one blossom facing full into the summer sun. In most species, the tiny flowers are one-half inch wide with five white to pink petals.

Characterized by soupspoon-shaped leaf blades, the round-leaved sundew is by far the most common species in most of New England. Spatulate-leaved sundew *(Drosera intermedia)*, with narrower blades, is more common in coastal southern New England, along with the local thread-leaved sundew *(D. filiformis)*, which is on the Massachusetts Watch List. Two other rare circumboreal species of calcareous fens, *D. anglica* and *D. linearis*, grow in a single site at Crystal Bog in Maine.

Habitat: *Bogs, cut banks, wet ravines*
Flowers: *July to August*
Status: *Fairly common throughout New England*

Round-Leaved Sundew *Drosera rotundifolia*

HARE'S-TAIL or COTTON GRASS
Eriophorum vaginatum ssp. *spissum*

The Cyperaceae or sedge family is the second largest family of flowering plants. As such, one would think that the sedges would be better known and appreciated than they are. Sedges are often taken lightly or even shunned by the amateur naturalist or botanist because, darn it, there are just so many of them and *they all look alike*. Hare's-tail is a happy and beautiful exception to the Gordian knot of sedgedom.

With a bright sun backlighting its brilliant white seed hairs, or seta, hare's-tail is a striking and readily identifiable beacon to any walker within yards of its bog habitat. These silky banners are entirely absent from some bogs and locally abundant in others. Good examples of cotton grass bogs occur on the south side of Mt. Adams and in the small isolated perched bogs below the summit of Mt. Washington.

Cotton grass is obviously a misnomer; its three-sided stem, or solid culm, is diagnostic for this and most other sedges. (Grasses are generally round stemmed and hollow; cotton is in the mallow family.) The scientific name *Eriophorum* describes the plant much better; it's taken from the Greek, meaning "wool-bearing."

This species has a single woolly head topping a leafless scape that can reach 3 feet in height. Other members of this genus bear multiple heads, though their silken seta are not as startling white as *Eriophorum vaginatum*.

Always an indicator of nutrient-poor, acidic waters, hare's-tail is much more common in the northern coniferous peatlands of Canada north to Baffin Bay, extending south only to Minnesota and the mountains of Pennsylvania. Its wispy brilliance is a welcome sight in autumn, enlivening the peat bogs long after most other flowering species have passed into senescence.

Habitat: *Acidic bogs*
Flowers: *July to October*
Status: *Uncommon*

Hare's-Tail or Cotton Grass   *Eriophorum vaginatum* ssp. *spissum*

SMALL PURPLE-FRINGED ORCHID
Platanthera psycodes

Sometimes called soldier's plume, this is one of six fringed orchids (sometimes called orchis) found in New England. Though they come in a range of colors, including the uncanny cantaloupe orange of a southern species, all share the finely cut lip, or labellum, the inverted petal characteristic of the orchid family. In purple-fringed orchids this lower petal is divided into three wide-spreading wings, explaining the fancied resemblance to a butterfly implied by the name *psycodes*.

The lower petal is designed not so much for butterflies as for their scale-winged cousins, the moths. Drawn to the fringed landing platform provided by the petal, the insects hover or rest while their long tongues unroll and lap the nectar contained in the petal's spur. In doing so, the moth's head brushes against the anthers just above the lip. Here rests a pollinia, a round bead of sticky pollen, ready to hitch a ride to the next flower. Thus genetic information is exchanged between different plants. And therein lies a botanical confusion of the first order.

The taxonomy of this group of orchids is complex and subject to debate by experts. Depending on the source you may find this plant referred to as *Platanthera psycodes*, or *Habenaria psycodes* var. *psycodes*. A close relative, the large purple-fringed orchid, may be found as *P. grandiflora*, or *H. fimbriata*, or *H. psycodes* var. *grandiflora*. In addition, there is a purple fringe-*less* orchid (accepted as a valid species *P.* [or *H.*] *peramoena*). And there are white versions of both the small and large purple-fringed orchids: forms *albiflora* (for both) or *nivalis* (for the large, if you lump the two species). These latter two must not be confused with the white prairie fringed orchid, *P.* or *H. leucophaea*, known only from one locale in New England.

Let's cut through this nomenclature nightmare, if possible. Seen side by side in the New England mountains, the small and large purple-fringed are easily separated by the size and the deeper color of the large. The small is more often found in open, wetland situations, often in grasses or even cattails, and usually in richer soils. The large is more likely in wet forest areas. The large on average blooms a couple weeks earlier than the small. For good measure, the best advice is that you head out with a metric rule during the purple-fringed season. Flowers with a lip less than 17 millimeters wide are those of the small purple-fringed.

Habitat: *Damp thickets, wet meadows*
Flowers: *Late July to August*
Status: *Uncommon*

Small Purple-Fringed Orchid   *Platanthera psycodes*

Lake Willoughby cliffs, Vermont

Connecticut River ledges, New Hampshire

CLIFFS, LEDGES,
AND TALUS SLOPES

The cackling calls of ravens add to the foreboding of the mineral-streaked cliffs rising from the shores of Vermont's Lake Willoughby. At least annually we take to this inhospitable terrain for a hazardous clamber up a loose rockslide to the base of the cliffs. Weirdly angled ledges serve as risers, leading up to the choice botanical locations—mossy rivulets, sodden crevices, clumps of hanging soil where some of New England's rarest flowers grow. The exhilaration of high places mixes with an attention to detail, and one must be wary of a misstep on the way to a clump of sweetbroom or a dainty native fleabane. Here, high above New England summer camps on the shores of a fjordlike lake, are plants of the far north in their southernmost home.

The plant communities of New England's rock outcrops—ledges, cliffs, and loose rock talus slopes—are determined by physical limitations that are not encountered in soil-covered forests and meadows. Sparse growth or nonexistent trees and shrubs lend an abundance of sunshine to the open rocks. A south-facing ledge might be able to support plants far north of their usual range. Where water flows over the rocks a loose peaty soil may form, supporting luxurious gardens of colorful, fleshy plants. Where water runs off or disappears into the jumbled mass of talus rock, dry (xeric) conditions prevail and tough, wiry plants may grow. Whatever the conditions, the thin soil cover with its premium on nutrients makes for a community far different from that located only a few feet away in the woods.

The composition of the bedrock determines the nature of these out-crops: sheer, sloping, broken. Bedrock also determines the chemical nature of the substrate, and certain types of rock support peculiar plants adapted to these limited habitats. Although New England soils are famous for the stones left embedded in them by ice age glaciers, simple rock outcrops are relatively rare in the region. When found they are often cultural artifacts—the result of recent logging or fires—where natural communities may not yet be reestablished.

Geology has determined that New England's rock outcrops vary markedly from place to place. The Lake Willoughby cliffs share with the heights of Smugglers Notch a sufficient amount of calcium in their thin soils—and a sufficiently cold climate—to support species like the mountain saxifrages, otherwise found in arctic areas of Canada. Since talus slopes—where the loose rocks are always (if slowly) on the move—are inimical to tree growth, they may share the species of the cliffs. Thus, rare species may be found growing in roadside gravels at the base of the slope.

Southern plants of calcareous soils appear primarily in the Berkshires and Taconics. Bartholomew's Cobble in southwestern Massachusetts is an outstanding example of this community (and highly accessible, as a public trust). Scarcely mountainous, the area consists of open limy cliffs above a pastoral meadow. In these secretive dells under a sparse forest shade grow plants like harebell also found in alpine meadows and, in particular, a number of rare and unusual ferns, such as cliff brake, wall rue, and walking fern. Atop the outcrops sprawl the lavender spring blossoms of purple clematis.

Rich, warm mountain ridges extend northward and up the Connecticut River valley. Wantastiquet in New Hampshire is a good example. Here more xeric conditions support communities similar to those seen in New York or Pennsylvania. Wild columbine is a common plant of these sun-washed ledges.

New England's granite core lies in the White Mountains and other scattered locations. Here a peculiar erosional process called exfoliation produces both sheer arching cliffs (as seen on Cannon Mountain) and domelike summits. The ledges of the latter, so easy to scramble up, are home to a few distinctive plants, most notably the silverling, a subalpine mountain endemic of the region. Talus slopes below soaring cliffs support scrubby growths of crowberries and laurels, along with young birch and mountain alder able to grow on still-shifting ground. Water is at a premium on talus, as well as on some dry ledges where low blueberries add taste to the reward of the view.

Certain rock formations are particularly unusual in New England. Volcanic rocks are of great age and have been much altered by time. These basalt, traprock, rhyolite, and other volcanic outcrops are known for some unusual plants, including the rock harlequin with its delicate pink-and-yellow blossoms. Serpentine bedrock is even more limited in the region, appearing in only a handful of outcrops. Deep mantle rock, serpentine has a complicated chemistry lacking the usual plant nutrients but high in metals. The resulting plant community is an area of sparse and stunted vegetation. A few plants have adapted to such locales; serpentine sandwort has a single United States station on Vermont's Haystack Mountain.

Tucked away in mountain hollows and broad river valleys are those microhabitats called calcareous seeps. Here lime-rich water percolates along shallow bedrock outcrops, supporting a mat of low vegetation that thrives on the calcium, dampness, and abundant light. An indicator plant of calcareous seeps, the grass-of-parnassus is a fall flower with distinctive round basal leaves. In the deepest of soils formed over these seeps, the showy lady's-slipper appears, while on riverside ledges scoured by ice, grow some of our most interesting flowers. For beauty and botanical interest, these are the rarest of our natural rock gardens.

EARLY SAXIFRAGE
Saxifraga virginiensis

Even as snowmelt cascades down bedrock outcrops and rocky ledges in mid-April, the early saxifrage seems literally to burst from the stony face of the mountains to reward the intrepid early spring hiker.

The 1-foot-high leafless scape topped with a corymb of tiny flowers rises from a basal rosette of spatulate, slightly dentate leaves. The rosette forms the previous autumn and weathers the severe New England winter. This photosynthetic jump on other deciduous species probably explains why the plant has the energy to muster a relatively impressive inflorescence so early in the year.

The round-topped corymb of five-petaled white flowers (green in form *chlorantha*) is a busy place for bumblebees and moths, undoubtedly hard put to find sources of nectar and pollen so early in the flowering season.

Early saxifrage has the unusual habit of cleaving a foothold in seemingly impenetrable rock crevices with its perennial rootstock. This may have led to its Latin name; *saxum* means "rock" and *frangere* means "to break," hence the common moniker, rockbreaker. At least one author states that the name is also a reminder of the ancient Doctrine of Signatures, which maintained that a plant's shape, color, or general habit illustrated how it could be used medicinally. An infusion of the juice of early saxifrage was once used to help break up kidney stones.

Habitat: *Rocks, ledges*
Flowers: *Mid-April to May*
Status: *Common in western New England (uncommon in central New Hampshire and Maine)*

Early Saxifrage   *Saxifraga virginiensis*

PURPLE CLEMATIS
Clematis occidentalis

Flowers of the buttercup family, which includes purple clematis, have the dubious distinction of being considered the most primitive of herbs in the subclass of dicotyledons. Science views the spiral arrangement of the numerous flower parts as typical of early plants. Many members of the family have poorly developed petals, transitional with the stamens. The sepals (green and leaflike in many other plants) are large and brightly colored, taking on the petals' traditional role. In this condition they are properly called tepals. The four tepals of purple clematis are a delicate violet that catches the eye wherever they arise from this climbing plant's mass of greenery.

Easily distinguished from the other wild *Clematis* species by its large, solitary flowers, purple clematis's four tepals remain partly closed, forming a tulip-shaped bell that hangs among the three-parted leaves. Flowers give way to fuzzy seed heads, each female style becoming a feathery fruit that lofts the seeds skyward.

The related white-flowered virgin's bower *(Clematis virginiana)* is a conspicuous roadside plant throughout New England, almost weedy in its aggressive growth. At one time the peppery roots of virgin's bower were ground and placed in the nostrils of tired horses to revive them, giving special meaning to the alternate name traveler's joy. No such medicinal use is recorded for purple clematis, which like other buttercup family members may contain poisonous oils.

Most of the 35 or so North American species of clematis are vines that clamber over rocks and trees under the twisting grip of their leaf stalks. The name *clematis*, coined by the ancient botanist Dioscorides, derives from the root word *clema*, meaning "a shoot." All three New England species grow up over their surroundings, usually where they find semishade for roots and full sun for flowering branches.

In the wild, clematis has a restricted New England range, dictated by its taste for the sweet soils of limestone regions. Northern Maine and Vermont have widespread colonies, with only spotty occurrences in the Granite State. The popularity of the vine among collectors and gardeners has led to its listing in Massachusetts—where it grows in the Connecticut River valley and Berkshires—as a species of special concern.

Habitat: *Limy riverbanks, ledges, rocky woods*
Flowers: *May to mid-June*
Status: *Uncommon; special concern species in Massachusetts*

Purple Clematis   *Clematis occidentalis*

PURPLE MOUNTAIN-SAXIFRAGE
Saxifraga oppositifolia

The most unusual of our native rockbreakers is the purple mountain-saxifrage, a low-growing, matted plant with limy encrustations on its tiny, rounded leaves. Most of the saxifrages have white flowers, often clustered at the end of long, leafless stems. This plant has a single, showy purple flower at the end of each stem; the stem is densely covered with overlapping paired leaves. The alternate names twinleaf saxifrage and French knot plant both refer to this unique arrangement of leaves, which makes the plant difficult to confuse with others in its rocky habitat.

The name *Saxifraga*, meaning "rockbreaker," recalls the Doctrine of Signatures whereby signals placed in the plants by the Creator signified their pharmaceutical use. Besides the plants' ability to grow in rock crevices, the grainy bulbs of some species look like kidney stones. By luck this medicinal doctrine sometimes worked, ensuring the celebrity of its practitioners, who believed they were something better than medicine men.

Saxifrage family members in New England's mountains are mostly limited to areas with limy soils. *Saxifraga, Parnassia,* and *Mitella* are all typical of the rich forests of the Connecticut Valley and the Green Mountain foothills. The only genus common in acidic and circumneutral soils is *Tiarella,* the foamflower. The mountain-saxifrages (purple, white, and yellow) are circumpolar plants—their distribution girdles the northern reaches of the globe. The plant of Vermont ledges also grows high on the mountains of Wyoming and Washington, the tundra of Alaska and Canada, and the cliffs of the Alps.

Seeing the color show of purple mountain-saxifrage in New England can be quite an excursion. Put on your climbing shoes and find the flower clinging to the wet ledges and loose talus slopes of Smugglers Notch and Lake Willoughby in northern Vermont; but be sure to arrive in the brief week or so of flowering or you'll miss the display. The plant is also widely planted in rock gardens where the cultivars are trained to bloom longer and larger, as in the purple-crimson sport called Splendens. Still, there is no better place to view the plant than from the high cliffs of Mt. Mansfield where you can look down on patches of "purple mountain-saxifrage above the fruited plain."

Habitat: *Calcareous ledges, cliffs*
Flowers: *Mid-May to early June*
Status: *Rare; Vermont only*

Purple Mountain-Saxifrage   *Saxifraga oppositifolia*

YELLOW MOUNTAIN-SAXIFRAGE
Saxifraga aizoides

Botanizing in the high peaks of New England is an exhilarating experience; at times it can be downright dangerous. But the thrill of finding a little-known plant growing on a precarious ledge far off the beaten track can overcome the trepidations of even the most fainthearted flatland botanist. The rare plants of the Lake Willoughby cliffs of northern Vermont present such a challenge.

Hundreds of feet above the bottomless blue of Lake Willoughby rises the daunting talus slope and sheer limestone rampart of Mt. Pisgah. The rare plant community of these slippery slopes has intrigued botanists for well over a century and a half. Alphonso Wood in his 1846 *Woods Classbook of Botany* writes of botanizing "500 feet above Willoughby Lake."

The plants that cling to life in this forbidding habitat are calciphilic, meaning they grow in limestone areas high in calcium; in normally acidic New England, these species are found in very few locales. Three of the most elusive of these cliff dwellers are the dwarf mountain-saxifrages: purple mountain-saxifrage, live-long saxifrage, and the brilliant yellow mountain-saxifrage.

Wonderfully adapted to the harsh environment in which it grows, the yellow mountain-saxifrage, like its other two soul mates, actually exudes encrusted lime from pores located at the tips of its needle-shaped leaves. Sharing the "rockbreaking" morphology of other members of this family, the flowers rise from tight basal offshoots no more than 3 or 4 inches above the rocky substrate.

The five-petaled flowers are bright yellow to orange and present a sunny visage to the weary climber laden with camera equipment and backpack. Against the backdrop of the gray rock face, the flowers seem all the more cheering and surprisingly large for such a diminutive plant; they seem a reflection of the bright Vermont sun, the floral faces following the sun's path in a heliotropic gaze.

Yellow mountain-saxifrage flowers from July to the end of August, later than the other two dwarf saxifrages. It is circumpolar in distribution, found in alpine areas of Europe, Asia, and North America. Rare in New England, it grows only in two northern Vermont counties, as well as in western New York State.

Habitat: *Limy cliffs, ledges, and talus* Flowers: *July and August*
Status: *Rare; northern Vermont only*

Yellow Mountain-Saxifrage   *Saxifraga aizoides*

DWARF PRIMROSE
Primula mistassinica

First described by the botanist Michaux in 1792 from specimens collected at Lake Mistassini in Quebec, dwarf primrose is one of only two *wild* New England representatives of a group of plants common in gardens. Now and then one of these garden varieties will pop up in a lawn, but dwarf primrose and the other native species *(Primula laurentiana)* must be sought in the scattered locations in northern Maine and Vermont where they thrive, relics of much larger populations that now occur only in the true boreal forests to the north.

Grown in English gardens since Elizabethan times, the primroses are boreal and alpine flowers, numbering perhaps 500 species worldwide, typically growing in rock crevices and boggy places. Parry's primrose of the Rocky Mountains is a well-known example of the plants' uncultivated beauty beside mountain rills. The names *Primula* and primrose both refer to the early spring (*primus* in Latin) blooming of the garden primrose, which is sometimes collected as a wild escape.

Our dwarf primrose (sometimes called bird's-eye primrose) shares the pink to lavender petal color of its western cousin. The basal rosette of leaves is small at flowering time, enlarging later, typically emerging out of shoreline gravels or from a moist crack in a cliff or ledge. The tiny flowers are tubular and five lobed, with the center typically yellow (thus the name bird's-eye). There is a white form *leucantha*, most common in Newfoundland, and a variety *novaboracensis*, lacking the yellow eye, found in the north-central states.

In the more northerly reaches of the continent this is a common and widespread primrose with less specific habitat requirements than others. This distribution, along with genetic evidence, leads taxonomists to consider it similar to the ancestral species, persistent through the ice ages. Today's warmer climate and general lack of calcareous rocks in New England have left dwarf primrose with a tenuous hold on existence in our mountains. It appears on the rare plant list in both states where it occurs. Today it may be more common (and overlooked) in Maine than when it was listed in the federal register as a candidate for Endangered Species Act protection.

Habitat: *Calcareous cliffs, talus, and shores*
Flowers: *Mid-May to June*
Status: *Rare; threatened species in Vermont*

Dwarf Primrose *Primula mistassinica*

SHRUBBY CINQUEFOIL
Potentilla fruticosa

Here's a plant that botanists can play the name game with—to ultimate confusion, or understanding. Carolus Linnaeus originally named it *Potentilla fruticosa* ("powerful shrubby plant"). Worldwide, scientists have assigned over 300 plant species to the genus *Potentilla*, even though the name originated with a sprawling coastal species said to have potent medicinal qualities. Taxonomic botanists have begun to question the lumping of these many plants into one genus. Some have now assigned our one shrubby species a new name, *Pentaphylloides floribunda*, meaning "many-flowered five-leaf," which is nothing if not descriptive.

The common name shrubby cinquefoil ("five-leaf") is also descriptive enough, as this is the only plant in the group with woody, shred-barked stems, which bear five-parted, toothless leaves. Since the leaves are pinnately compound (arranged like a ladder) rather than palmately (arranged like fingers) the cinquefoil synonym five-finger does not apply. But other common names are available. Golden hardhack is a reminder that the plant can become a nuisance when it grows in pastures where farmers are hard pressed to hack out woody vegetation.

Widdy is the name given to the plant in Newfoundland (we can't tell you why) whereas Alaskans call it tundra rose, a reminder that it shares the basic rose family pattern of five showy petals and numerous (in this case 25 to 30) stamens.

In New England's mountains, shrubby cinquefoil grows in the wild in the pastures of Massachusetts and Vermont where there's lime in the soil, and in isolated mountain stations on cliffs, ledges, and talus slopes (as at Smugglers Notch, Dilly Cliffs, and Huntington Ravine). More likely you will find it growing outside your hometown bank or in your own garden, under a number of names: Katherine Dykes, Moonlight, Tangerine, and Vilmoriniana.

Say this for shrubby cinquefoil, it has not lacked for human attention. It's a rose by every other name.

Habitat: *Ledges, talus, pastures, open wet areas*
Flowers: *June to September*
Status: *Uncommon*

Shrubby Cinquefoil   *Potentilla fruticosa*

THREE-TOOTHED CINQUEFOIL
Potentilla tridentata

Three-toothed cinquefoil grows in some of New England's harshest environments, from windswept sandplains and old dune ridges on Cape Cod to the summit of Mt. Washington. The similarities of coastal and alpine landscapes may not be obvious, but their threadbare soils of sterile sands and gravels share a number of plant species, including this tough little member of the rose family.

A common element of the alpine and subalpine floral community, this species of cinquefoil is distinctive because of its white flowers and three-part leaves. Most other members of *Potentilla* have yellow flowers and five-part leaves (*cinque* in French meaning "five"). Each leathery evergreen leaflet is topped by three notches at its tip, hence its species name *tridentata* and colloquial name, trident cinquefoil. In autumn the undersides of the leaflets turn a rich burgundy red, contrasting nicely with the pale rocks or sands that serve as backdrop. Thus, wine leaf cinquefoil is another common name.

This plant has not only adapted to a wide range of regional habitats, it is also protean in form and function. In deeper soils and full sunlight on protected lower elevations it can grow to 18 inches in height and be quite leggy in aspect. On alpine rock summits, the three-toothed assumes a nearly prostrate form against the bare granitic rock face. In lowland situations it thrives in lawns, as at Lafayette Place in Franconia Notch.

Ranging from the tundra of Greenland south to the Appalachian peaks of Georgia, three-toothed cinquefoil is a handsome addition to the hardscrabble worlds of both seacoast and mountaintop.

Habitat: *Rocky and windswept outcrops*
Flowers: *June to August*
Status: *Common in appropriate habitats*

Three-Toothed Cinquefoil   *Potentilla tridentata*

ALPINE SWEETBROOM
Hedysarum alpinum

Also known as sweetvetch, this member of the pea family bears some resemblance to its weedy cousin, the roadside purple vetch. Among native peas are three similar-looking groups that are widespread in the western and northern parts of the continent: *Astragalus, Oxytropis,* and *Hedysarum.* Of the last, there are about 100 species worldwide, a few of which are shrubs, but most are bushy wildflowers like this one. Alpine sweetbroom is the only *Hedysarum* species to be found in New England, and even then only in a few widely scattered locations.

On the Vermont talus slopes and limy ledges where we have found this plant, it is a leafy mass of bright green foliage, with numerous stems bearing brightly colored racemes of drooping flowers in a distinctive shade of pink. In common with all pea family flowers, this one has an unusual structure consisting of a standard and a keel, lengthened in the direction of the flower's fall. The seeds that result from insects' encounters with the stamens (and styles) are contained in a loment, or pod, with constrictions between the seeds—like a pea pod pinched between the peas.

The healthy growth of sweetbroom depends, as in all members of the pea family, on the microscopic interaction of plant and bacteria at root level. Chemical compounds on the root hairs bind preferentially to surface molecules of the bacteria *Rhizobium* living in the soil. Once these germs infect the root, nodules are formed within which the bacteria live, exchanging nitrogen compounds for plant sugars. The production of nitrogenase in the bacteria requires a material that will bind oxygen. Using the DNA pattern in the plant cells and the heme-group molecules in the bacteria, the partnership produces leghemoglobin, similar to the substance in animal blood. This similarity is symbolized by the pink flesh tones of the root nodules.

In Alaska natives call sweetbroom Eskimo potato and collect the fleshy roots for eating raw or cooked. More important in the West is the plant's use by wildlife, especially grizzly bears, which seek this plant's roots as their chief springtime food. Although it requires some imagination, the image of a 700-pound grizzly tearing into the moist ground to uproot a sweetbroom is one of the vicarious pleasures of finding sweetbroom growing in wild New England locales.

Habitat: *Limy cliffs and riverbanks*
Flowers: *June to July*
Status: *Rare; northern Maine and Vermont only*

Alpine Sweetbroom *Hedysarum alpinum*

BLACK CROWBERRY
Empetrum nigrum

The crowberries are a tough family of subshrubs found in some of the severest habitats in New England, from rocky alpine slopes of Mt. Katahdin and Mt. Washington, to the windswept shoreline of Mt. Desert Island. The low sprawling habit and needlelike evergreen leaves are practical adaptations to the crowberries' harsh environment.

Empetraceae, the crowberry family, is a curious group strongly resembling the heaths (Ericaceae). M. L. Fernald in *Gray's Manual of Botany* describes the crowberries as "degenerate relation" to the heaths. Empetraceae is composed of only three genera, with the two others, *Corema* and *Ceratiola*, ranging along southern coastal areas. Black crowberry is the only true alpine tundra species, being found within 10 degrees of the North Pole.

Flowering in late May, its inconspicuous tiny purple flowers tucked into the tight leaf axils go largely unnoticed. Later in the summer the round black berries appear, sometimes in great numbers. Unlike other tasty alpine fruit such as bilberries and mountain cranberries, crowberries are dry and mealy. They are apparently quite palatable to ptarmigan and other arctic birds, who relish the fruit. The fruit's avian popularity is revealed in its other names such as curlewberry, crow-pea, and crake-berry.

Another close relative is the purple crowberry *(Empetrum eamesii* ssp. *atropurpureum)*, which supposedly has purple fruit and branches covered with densely matted hair. Fruit color and surfaces of new growth are extremely variable, which has led in the past to the lumping of both into a single species by many authors. Due to its having perfect flowers (containing both stamens and pistils), black crowberry is currently placed in a separate species from the unisexual purple crowberry. Both are found in essentially the same habitat, although the purple is considered much less common in the highest elevations.

Habitat: *Rocky ledges, mostly montane*
Flowers: *Late May to early June*
Status: *Uncommon; threatened species in New Hampshire*

Black Crowberry *Empetrum nigrum*

PALE CORYDALIS or ROCK HARLEQUIN
Corydalis sempervirens

In the wake of the clearcut logging that plundered the forests of New England's mountains around the turn of the past century, devastating fires swept over the slopes, fueled by dry branches and pitch-filled treetops. Hot, deep-burning fires sent accumulated centuries of forest soil up in smoke. To this day, some mountains once cloaked in forests are marked by stunted pioneer growths of paper birch or tangles of red spruce between open ledges. Here, as a tiny bright spot in this otherwise gloomy story of resource exploitation, we find the creation of ideal habitat for the delicate pink and yellow wildflower known as pale corydalis or rock harlequin.

Botanical manuals do not agree on the taxonomic placement of the oddly shaped flowers of the corydalis and related groups such as the bleeding hearts. Some botanists lump them with the regular flowers of the poppy family; others put all these four-petaled, spurred flowers into the fumitory family. The genus *Corydalis* has an upper, outer petal drawn into a spur at the back and spread into a hood at the front. Insects that properly enter the flower by the yellow-fronted entrance encounter the two inner petals and the hidden stamens, gathering pollen incidentally to their pursuit of the sweet nectar in the spur. Once fertilized the seeds are explosively discharged when the elastic walls of the seed capsule curl back.

Rock harlequin refers to the brightly colored flower, reminiscent of the gaudy clothing of the comic characters of pantomime. The scientific name *Corydalis* derives from the Greek word for the crested lark, for the fancied resemblance of the flower to this bird. There are blue and purple species of corydalis, which can be found in gardens, and several yellow species in the wild.

One of the latter, golden smoke or scrambled eggs *(Corydalis aurea)* is a western species known only from our Connecticut River and Champlain Valleys in Vermont, where it is listed as a threatened species. Unlike the pale corydalis, the climbing fumitory *(Adlumia fungosa)* has two spurs and is vinelike in habit, growing over moist rather than dry ledges. However, both can be found in widely scattered locations on lower mountains in New England in their preferred habitat, on the rocks.

Habitat: *Dry ledges, gravels, and open woods*
Flowers: *June to August*
Status: *Uncommon*

Pale Corydalis or Rock Harlequin   *Corydalis sempervirens*

GRASS-OF-PARNASSUS
Parnassia glauca

The Nine Muses of Mt. Parnassus in ancient Greek mythology were the goddesses devoted to the higher arts such as poetry, music, and oratory. They lived atop a peak in central Greece, high above the artists they inspired. While this may seem a rather lofty name for a small New England wildflower, grass-of-Parnassus is both handsome and different for many reasons.

Rising from a rosette of round, leathery leaves, the solitary flower is borne on a long 1- to 2-foot scape. The five white to cream-colored petals are intricately laced with green veins, quite unlike any flower in our area. Surrounding the ovary are five fertile stamens with normal, spore-producing anthers. Alternating between each stamen grow five more curious structures known as staminodia. These appendages are actually sterile stamens with three prongs cleft into what appears to be a standard anther; no pollen is produced by these staminodia, however, and the inquisitive botanist must wonder at their function. Perhaps these floral eunuchs are more noticeable and attractive to pollinators than the lower-profile fertile stamens.

Grass-of-Parnassus is not a grass but a member of the large and polymorphous saxifrage family. It typically grows in calcareous clay banks and spring seeps in wet meadows in northern and western New England. Nowhere is it common, but in the proper habitat it can be found locally in good numbers.

Grass-of-Parnassus adorns our landscape long after the majority of wildflowers have gone to seed, beginning in late summer and sometimes flowering well into October. Its eye-catching zebra blossoms, along with the fringed gentian, are the last of our native flora to inspire our muse until the following spring. Thus, it helps to shorten the winter ahead.

Habitat: *Calcareous banks and springy meadows*
Flowers: *Mid-August to early October*
Status: *Uncommon to rare; threatened species in New Hampshire*

Grass-of-Parnassus
Parnassia glauca

BOG CANDLE or LEAFY WHITE ORCHIS
Platanthera dilitata

The only conspicuous member of the orchid family that a hiker above tree line is likely to encounter in New England is the leafy white orchis, also called bog candle for its erect posture. Other than the almost mythical prairie fringed orchis of northern Maine, bog candle is the most impressive of the so-called rein orchids. A plant of protean form, it is sometimes a mere slender, unpretentious wand of half a foot in height; in its optimum habitat of seepy calcareous soils, however, this species presents a robust flower stalk measuring 3 feet with dozens of milk white flowers.

Bog candle frequently grows in marly roadside ditches in the northern portions of Maine, New Hampshire, and Vermont in late June, often with a close relative, the northern green orchis *(Platanthera hypoborea)*. Sharing the same habitat and often hybridizing, bog candle is readily distinguished from the northern green by the white, not green, flowers and its wonderful spicy scent of cloves. The hybrid, *P. media*, is often more vigorous and abundant than either parent species.

In mid-August, bog candle appears above tree line, where it can be found in the rills and freshets of the mist-enshrouded headwall of Tuckerman Ravine. Growing with arnica, purple-stemmed aster, pale painted cup, and sphagnum moss, bog candle lends a dignified, almost ghostly presence to these mucky seepages. More than most other orchids, bog candle loves the deep mire of a fen or seep (it was once placed in the genus *Limnorchis* or "marsh orchid").

More common in boreal regions than in the southern part of its range in the mountains of northern New Jersey and Pennsylvania, this orchid is found from Alaska to Newfoundland, where it is locally known as scent bottle for its unusual fragrance.

Habitat: *Fens, swamps, and spring seeps*
Flowers: *Mid-June to August*
Status: *Uncommon; threatened species in Massachusetts*

Bog Candle or Leafy White Orchis   *Platanthera dilitata*

MUSK FLOWER
Mimulus moschatus

Only recently recognized as a native member of our flora, the musk flower's natural range has been obscured by the ability of garden plants to seed into the wild. Technical manuals offer differing interpretations of its native haunts: Seymour's *Flora of New England* states that the plant was introduced from the south and west, while Fernald's *Gray's Manual of Botany* treats it as indigenous in Newfoundland, the Magdalen Islands, and northern Michigan, and introduced elsewhere. The Connecticut River valley occurrences of this distinctive yellow flower are now considered to be indigenous—a recognition, if not return, of the native. Although of little concern to amateurs, the question of whether a plant was part of the original flora of an area is vital to botanists wishing to protect the mix of species that time and the elements planted on the New England landscape.

Both musk flower and the smooth-leaved western species *(Mimulus guttatus)* are popular colonizers in rock gardens, where they thrive in moist areas. One of these appeared spontaneously in the historic alpine garden at the John Hay estate in New Hampshire a few years ago, much to the puzzlement of the gardener, who had not seen it in his two decades of work.

Although both the common name and the species name refer to a musky odor, this is not always present in the plant. Characteristic is the clammy hairiness of the stems and leaves, rising from underground runners to form sprawling colonies. Members of the genus *Mimulus* are often called monkey flowers for the imagined resemblance of the flaring corolla to the grinning face of a monkey. This quality—reflected in the name *Mimulus* variously translated as "little buffoon," "mime," "ape," or "mask"—is far more apparent in the purple species of lakeshores.

When probed by bird beak or bumbling insect, the unequal lobes of the flower come together, the better to brush some pollen off onto the visitor. The name spring-seep monkey flower used in the West for the yellow species is appropriate for New England flowers as well. Look for them spread out across wet ground and ledges in the lime rock country of Vermont, Massachusetts, and New Hampshire.

Habitat: *Spring seeps and wet ledges*
Flowers: *June to August*
Status: *Rare; endangered species in New Hampshire; threatened species in Massachusetts*

Musk Flower *Mimulus moschatus*

YELLOW RATTLE
Rhinanthus minor and *Rhinanthus borealis*

An unassuming little annual of northern fields and mountain meadows, yellow rattle is named for its swollen, almost orbicular, toothed calyx, which inflates in fruit to produce a seed-rattling pod. The sunny yellow, arching "parrot beak" of its upper lip protrudes shyly from the calyx envelope, somewhat like another member of the figwort family, turtlehead. This beak, known botanically as a "galea," gives it a genus name, which in Greek means "snout flower."

Yellow rattle is often overlooked in flower, as it peers out from the taller grasses and forbs of the fields, both wet and dry, which it favors. It is more noticeable in fruit, with its balloonish calyx filled with round seeds rattling audibly as a walker brushes past (this should not be confused with rattle box, a coastal plain species of no relation). In England, a similar species is affectionately known as penny rattle and rattle bags.

Some botanists question the native status of yellow rattle in the southern part of its range (coastal areas of lower New England). Most manuals relegate it to adventive or even introduced status south of its boreal range of northern New England and upper New York.

Other authors divide the genus into two species, with *Rhinanthus borealis* of the northern mountains described as having wider leaves while *R. minor* typically has a sharply pointed, narrow-based leaf. For many years an introduced species, *R. major*, with larger flowers grew in the fields of Plymouth, Massachusetts. This possible relic of the Pilgrims is no longer found in America's hometown, but hikers on Mts. Mansfield or Washington can still hear the familiar rattle of its American cousins.

Habitat: *Alpine meadows, fields, or roadsides*
Flowers: *June and July*
Status: R. minor *occasional at lower elevations;* R. borealis *rare, in New Hampshire only*

Yellow Rattle *Rhinanthus minor*

HAREBELL
Campanula rotundifolia

The stone terraces, boulder fields, and rock crevices of the Alpine Garden below Mt. Washington in the late alpine summer can seem a rugged place for so delicate a wildflower as harebell. Large bell flowers nod on impossibly thin, threadlike stems, and the plant grows where soil is scarce and the wind howls shrilly in late August.

A circumboreal species that grows in alpine areas and on rock ledges in the higher elevations of New England's mountains, harebell has been admired by hikers for generations, its stunning blue blossoms unlike any other color seen in the rugged tundra. To our eyes, the alpine form of this species seems a deeper shade of purple-blue than the lower-elevation populations. There is indeed much variation in this species, with true arctic plants rarely growing over 8 inches in height, with one to three flowers per plant. Harebells growing below tree line can grow to 2 feet with multiple blossoms. Whereas some authors recognize an arctic variety, M. L. Fernald, writing in *Gray's Manual of Botany*, dismisses these differences as mere adaptations to the vicissitudes of weather and climate.

Despite its great beauty, harebell is miserably named, both colloquially and scientifically; the *hare* in harebell not making a lot of sense (few hares are found in this plant's habitat) and the Latin specific name *(rotundifolia)* referring to the round basal leaves, which wither and die before the plant's blossoming time. The genus name is more apt, meaning "little bell." Other more accurately descriptive common names include mountain bluebells, bluebells of Scotland, and witch's bells.

Habitat: *Alpine tundra; limy ledges at low elevations*
Flowers: *Late July to August*
Status: *Uncommon*

Harebell *Campanula rotundifolia*

Alpine lawn, above Huntington Ravine

Alpine flora, Mt. Washington

THE ALPINE ZONE

Tuckerman Ravine, August. All remnant snowbanks have disappeared, but this year's meltwaters still slicken the cliffs and splash down gray rock staircases in this most celebrated of New England's glacial cirques. Along peat-bordered rills, beds of yellow arnica and purple asters crowd for blooming space; here and there white bog candle orchids rise on long stems, while creamy painted cups huddle beside fringes of stunted evergreens. The typical image of New England—white church, green meadow, dark forest—is challenged at these heights by the breathtaking vertical sweep of alpine country and the limitless horizons beyond the peaks.

From the Knife Edge of Katahdin deep in the Maine woods, to the Great Gulf of New Hampshire's Presidential Range, across the valley country to the Chin of Mt. Mansfield high above Vermont's farmlands, tiny islands of arctic-alpine vegetation thrive in the harshest of climates. Each year some unprepared hiker discovers, too often with fatal results, that though only a three-hour drive from Boston, Mt. Washington's weather is like that of Hudson's Bay. Sky-flung islands of broken rock exposed to year-round snowfall, our alpine areas preserve a scene much like that which dominated New England's landscape at the end of the Ice Age, 12,000 years ago. Yet the remnant is vanishingly small, with New Hampshire's 8 square miles of alpine country the largest of the lot.

Compare the plants included in this book with those found in a similar work on Alaskan or Rocky Mountain wildflowers. Chances are that the same species, or a close relative, is found in those more celebrated mountain worlds. Walk the tundra at Denali National Park at 2,000 feet elevation and you will encounter some of the same plants that grow at 5,500 feet in New England: Lapland rosebay, harebell, moss campion, alpine azalea, bog bilberry—all at home on both sides of the continent. Emergence and convergence explain the similarities. As the last land to be released from the glacial deep freeze, the high mountains emerged devoid of soil. Great heaps of frost-shattered rock, called felsenmeer, or cliffs plucked sheer by rivers of ice, offer scant root-hold for trees. Onto these rocky outposts converge most of North America's major storm tracks, bringing almost constant damp, biting arctic cold and fierce onslaughts of wind-driven snow and ice.

In this environment some lowland plants eke out a reduced lifestyle: fir and spruce trees a hundred or more years old stand a few feet tall in shrubby tendrils of krummholz. Some plants exist at high elevations in varieties slightly different from those found below; alpine bluets or innocence is a good example. All-purpose alien weeds like devil's paintbrush follow the roads and trails, lodging in tire and boot treads for the journey to the high peaks. But the alpine zone is dominated by plants that have the competitive advantage in an environment stressed by wind, cold, acidity, and lack of soil nutrients.

Arctic-alpine species share a wide array of evolutionary traits that make them fit to the land they colonize. Many grow low to the ground, where the temperatures are dramatically warmer and wind velocities far less powerful. Diapensia is perhaps the best example of this characteristic, its leaf mound almost rocklike in its toughness. Alpine flowers, though small by lowland standards, are often all out of proportion to the size of their stems and leaves. Much of the alpine plant's energy-creating photosynthetic activity is used for this prodigious blossoming, calculated to maximize the attraction to pollinators. The early spring (that is, late *calendar* spring) flower show in places like the Alpine Garden draws hundreds of eager viewers and thousands of hungry insects.

Specialized microhabitats exist throughout the alpine zone and are co-opted by certain species. The Robbins' cinquefoil grows on a frost-heaved pavement of schistose gravel on an ancient erosional surface high on the shoulder of Mt. Monroe. A more generalized adaptation is the tough, leathery leaves found in many alpine species, leaves that can get an early start on photosynthesis when snows melt away *and* withstand the beating of windblown ice needles and temperatures at minus 40 degrees.

The very conditions that alpine wildflowers embrace have kept humans from exploiting this landscape as a year-round habitat. Still, the popularity of these high-country islands of tundra have led to their protection, and paradoxically, continued threats. In 1911 the Presidential Range was included in the White Mountain National Forest, Katahdin is the centerpiece of the privately protected Baxter State Park, and Mt. Mansfield rises in a vast state forest. Yet auto roads ascend both Mansfield and Washington, as well as Greylock and Ascutney to the south. On pleasant summer days the trails on any of these mountains can look like the line at a busy grocery store. Trampling threatens a few rare plants; far more dangerous is the development that hikers demand: an established overlook, a hikers' cabin, a visitor center—each takes priceless square feet of an extremely limited habitat.

Peaks without large alpine areas, such as Maine's Sugarloaf Mountain, could lose what little they have to ski developments, if their critical resources are overlooked or ignored.

Conservationists are educating the hiking public and casual tourists about the fragility of the alpine zone. Physical protection of some sites is being accomplished by rerouting trails, hiring ridge runners, and placing informational signs. Critical areas programs identify the remaining alpine country. Interestingly, there are a few mountain summits that boast alpine species *because of* human disturbance. The mountain sandwort flowers that grace the summit of Mt. Monadnock are growing there because fires, purposely set, burned away the soil and set back the successional clock to a postglacial alpine stage, on a peak that was once forested. This is not to suggest that we burn off mountains to create alpine tundra; it does suggest that unexpected results are to be expected from thoughtless human actions. What will our reliance on the internal combustion engine and the consequent global warming mean for the alpine outposts of New England?

DIAPENSIA
Diapensia lapponica

There is no plant better adapted to the brutal climate of the alpine tundra than diapensia, a seemingly delicate wildflower, which thrives in New England's most brutal mountain climates.

Peeking out from the microhabitat afforded by the tiniest rock crevice or forming convex mounds or cushions, this diminutive subshrub amazingly blooms well before almost any other alpine species, sometimes flowering in late May when snowstorms and subzero temperatures are still very real threats above tree line. Its milk white, five-lobed campanulate corolla is familiar only to those hardy enough to visit the Alpine Garden or Bigelow Lawn when the weather can still turn deadly.

A mounded colony of diapensia in full flower is a delightful sight, with the individual flowers so symmetrical and regular in design that they fit the stereotype of a child's first depiction of a flower. The corolla is quite deciduous, often more commonly seen lying intact on the ground than on the plant.

The tiny diapensia family is composed of only six genera, with *Diapensia lapponica* the only member of the family and genus found in New England. It is closely related to pixie moss *(Pyxidanthera barbulata)* of the New Jersey Pine Barrens. Some authors place the *Diapensias* in the heath family, but the stamens in *Diapensias* are free, not attached to the corolla as in the heaths.

A truly arctic-alpine species found only on the world's highest peaks and most formidable tundras, diapensia is locally common in the Presidential Range and on Mt. Katahdin and rare on Mt. Mansfield, with another isolated occurrence on Mt. Marcy in New York.

Habitat: *Bare gravelly ledges in the alpine zone*
Flowers: *Late May to June*
Status: *Locally common in limited habitat; endangered species in Vermont; special concern species in Maine*

Diapensia   *Diapensia lapponica*

LAPLAND ROSEBAY
Rhododendron lapponicum

Inch for inch, there is no more spectacular blossom in the alpine zone than Lapland rosebay. Bursting from the tightly packed, tiny branchlets, the three to five royal purple flowers measure over an inch across, with stamens and pistil arching out well beyond the flaring petal lobes. The flowers appear huge in proportion to the rest of the plant. Indeed, Lapland rosebay seems to almost disappear after its brief flowering period of approximately June 15 to June 30. The oversized flowers and early (for the alpine zone) blossoming are adaptations to the short growing season; it takes more warmth and time to form ripe seeds than to open a flower.

Lapland rosebay is one of the true arctic-alpine species found in New England. It is circumpolar, growing commonly in the tundra of Greenland, Canada, and Alaska, as well as on the higher peaks of Europe and Asia. In our region it is found only on Mts. Washington and Katahdin, with small numbers hanging on at Mt. Marcy in the Adirondacks. There is also a tiny disjunct population in the Dells of Wisconsin.

One of the characteristic "cushion" plants of the felsenmeer, Lapland rosebay forms low mounds of tightly coiled branches, mixing almost indistinguishably with diapensia and alpine azalea. The thick, scaly evergreen leaves are highly adapted to deflect the desiccating winds and strong sunlight of the arctic-alpine zone.

There are few plants on earth that can grow in the conditions that this tough little heath not only endures but thrives in. A hike through the Alpine Garden below the Washington summit in mid- to late June is unforgettable. The deep pinks of alpine azalea and moss campion, white of diapensia, and gaudy purple of Lapland rosebay create a dazzling palette of color in the otherwise drab fellfield. It is reason enough to scale the highest peak in the Northeast.

Habitat: *Rocky to peaty alpine soils*
Flowers: *Mid- to late June*
Status: *Locally common in the Presidential Range; endangered species in Maine; special concern species in New Hampshire*

Lapland Rosebay   *Rhododendron lapponicum*

ALPINE AZALEA
Loiseleuria procumbens

In a land of Lilliputian floral beauties, none is more diminutive than the alpine azalea. Barely a quarter of an inch high, this "shrub" has evergreen leaves that are shiny and revolute, or in-rolled, to diminish the amount of surface exposed to subfreezing temperatures and howling winds. The minute and delicate flowers have five-lobed white to pink corollas peaking straight up, barely higher than the glossy leaves. Unlike other azaleas, its stamens are not exserted beyond the petals. Even 100-mile-an-hour winds raise not a quiver from this procumbent alpine heath.

Like its fellfield counterparts, diapensia and Lapland rosebay, this tiniest of azaleas opens during the first wave of alpine flowering in early to mid-June. This leaves the greater part of the growing season for ripe fruit formation and energy storage for the next flowering year.

Alpine azalea has a slightly wider New England range than Lapland rosebay, being found in both the Presidential and Franconia Ranges, as well as on Mt. Katahdin in Maine, where it is officially listed as a state endangered species. It is truly arctic-alpine, ranging from Greenland to Alaska in North America and within the Arctic Circle in Europe and Asia.

Habitat: *Alpine tundra and fellfields*   Flowers: *June to early July*
Status: *Locally common in alpine New Hampshire; endangered species in Maine; threatened species in New Hampshire*

MOSS CAMPION
Silene acaulis var. *exscapa*

The dense mats of tiny, imbricated leaves and ¼-inch-wide flowers of this circumboreal, alpine-arctic species are a tough find amid the more abundant and showy inhabitants of the alpine zone. Convergent evolution is evident in moss campion—its dwarf cushion form and tufts of lance-shaped leaves superficially resemble such arctic-alpine species as alpine azalea, Lapland rosebay, and diapensia. Moss campion's attractive blossoms are distinctively of the Caryophyllaceae (Pink) family, though, not of the alpine zone's more common Ericaceae (Heath) family.

The five-petaled, pale pink or lavender flowers have a distinctive notch at the summit of each petal, the flowers solitary on a short stalk (or stalkless) nestled in the leaves. Moss campion may open only sporadically, though impressive "flower-carpet" displays can be seen in some years in late June or early July. This tough plant resembles a coarse moss when not in flower.

Habitat: *Alpine tundra and fellfields*   Flowers: *Late June to early July*
Status: *Local to rare on Mt. Washington above tree line; threatened in New Hampshire*

Alpine Azalea   *Loiseleuria procumbens*

Moss Campion   *Silene acaulis* var. *exscapa*

BOG BILBERRY
Vaccinium uliginosum var. *alpinum*

For the hungry hiker above tree line, there is no dearth of wild fruit in the alpine zone at the right season. Mountain cranberry and wren's egg cranberry, baked-apple berry, alpine bistort, and two species of blueberry provide a high altitude banquet for anyone choosing to sample these trailside nibbles. To our minds, however, none compares with the bog bilberry, a fat and juicy member of the blueberry tribe. The comparatively large blue fruits are sweet with none of the seediness of huckleberries. In a good year with plenty of moisture, the Alpine Garden on Mt. Washington is loaded with luscious bilberries from mid- to late August.

This low, somewhat matted shrub is the most common member of the heath family (Ericaceae) in the alpine zone. There are actually two closely related species known as bilberries: bog and dwarf (*Vaccinium caespitosum*). Bog bilberry has four-parted flowers with thick, entire-edged leaves whereas dwarf bilberry's flowers are five-parted with thin, finely toothed leaves. Although both produce juicy fruit, bog bilberry seems a bit sweeter to some palates.

Bog bilberry is widespread in arctic-alpine zones throughout the Northern Hemisphere, including Eurasia, Greenland, Alaska, and New England's highest peaks. Though common enough above tree line in New England, both bilberries occasionally grow at sea level in the Canadian maritime provinces.

Habitat: *Alpine tundra, gravelly soils*
Flowers: *June to July*
Status: *Common within its limited habitat*

Dwarf Bilberry flower   *Vaccinium caespitosum*

Bog Bilberry fruit   *Vaccinium uliginosum* var. *alpinum*

MOUNTAIN CRANBERRY
Vaccinium vitis-idaea

Of all the wild fruits found in the arctic-alpine zone, none makes as tasty a jelly or jam as the mountain cranberry. An attractive evergreen heath, mountain cranberry is well known to Laplanders in northern Europe who make it into lingonberry jam. Its scarlet fruits, while small, grow in clusters and yield readily to a hiker's gentle coaxing. Somewhat insipid if eaten right off the plant, they sweeten considerably if picked just after the first hard frost or snowmelt. Many wild food naturalists actually prefer this to the cultivated cranberries, which are often the product of insecticide and herbicide application by corporate, agricultural megacombines.

A circumpolar species found in most of the world's alpine areas, mountain cranberry is locally common above tree line on many of the high peaks of Maine, New Hampshire, and Vermont but, strangely, not in the Adirondacks of New York. It extends south to Mt. Greylock in western Massachusetts, where it clings to existence along the auto road. A lonely southernmost station in Granby, Connecticut, and a small colony in Danvers, Massachusetts, are now believed extirpated.

Mountain cranberry is attractive not only in fruit but also in flower; its four-lobed corolla ranges from light pink to the almost solid red pictured here. Flowering from mid-June to July, the fruits are ready for eating in late August. Loaded with vitamin C, mountain cranberry may be sampled as a fine trail snack.

Habitat: *Rocky summits*
Flowers: *Mid-June to mid-July*
Status: *Locally common north; endangered species in Massachusetts and Connecticut*

Mountain Cranberry   *Vaccinium vitis-idaea*

MOSS PLANT
Cassiope hypnoides

Moss plant, more poetically known as Cassiope, is one of the most delicate members of the so-called snowbank community in the rock crevices of New England's highest peaks. Colonizing wet fissures in the headwalls of the Great Gulf and Tuckerman Ravine, moss plant stays protected and unassuming until snowmelt ensues in late June or early July. Then its nodding bell-shaped blossoms open by the hundreds, enlivening the dark rock refugias with a cascade of white-and-pink flowers.

Convergent evolution is wonderfully illustrated by the mosslike leaves and habit of this tiny heath. Never growing higher than 2 or 3 inches, the plant's evergreen acicular leaves arranged around the creeping stems closely resemble a moss; indeed, when *Cassiope* is not in flower, most hikers mistake this plant for its nonvascular look-alike (the species' epithet means "like a hypnum," a well-known moss).

The closed campanulate flowers hang singly from a slender blood red peduncle. The five sepals, also scarlet, grip the base of the flower like the claws gripping the ball seen on the legs of old bathtubs.

A circumpolar alpine species, *Cassiope* grows in a very few places in New England, principally in moist ravine headwalls of Mt. Washington, Great Gulf, and Mt. Katahdin. It is not found on Mt. Mansfield. It is listed as endangered in Maine.

Cassiopeia was the mother of Andromeda in Greek mythology, and although her treatment of her daughter left something to be desired, this wonderful plant does not deserve the other name sometimes used by unromantic botanists: *Harrimanella*, named after American railroad tycoon Edward H. Harriman.

Habitat: *Snowmelt ravines, alpine headwalls*
Flowers: *Late June to July*
Status: *Rare; endangered species in Maine; threatened species in New Hampshire*

Moss Plant   *Cassiope hypnoides*

MOUNTAIN HEATH
Phyllodoce caerulea

Looking like a refugee from the great heaths of the Scottish highlands, mountain heath or heather is a highly colored member of the dwarf shrub community of the arctic-alpine zone. With nodding purple to mauve urn-shaped flowers and needlelike, evergreen leaves, this plant appears to borrow from both the ericads and the conifers. Indeed, the old species epithet was *taxifolia*, meaning "yew-leaved," a much more appropriate name than the accepted *caerulea* meaning "sky blue."

Mountain heath is an obligate member of the alpine community of northern New England, growing with a prostrate, creeping habit in the same peaty snowmelt crevices where *Cassiope* is found. Its range is restricted to the highest peaks of the Presidential and Franconia Ranges, where it is most commonly encountered on the east side of Mt. Washington and in scattered locations on Mt. Lafayette. It is quite rare on Mt. Katahdin and absent entirely from Mt. Mansfield.

Hikers hoping to catch a glimpse of this somewhat elusive little heath often find only the upturned and erect seed capsules on the elongated pedicels, for it is one of the earliest alpine wildflowers to bloom, often opening even as the snow melts around it in mid-June.

Although scientific names are in most instances far more appropriate and accurate than colloquial names, this is not the case for either the genus or species name for mountain heath. The *caerulea* misses the mark as to the purplish floral color and the genus is named for a sea nymph from Virgil's *Aeneid*, an allusion far removed from the windswept ravines that mountain heath calls home.

Habitat: *Alpine meadows and headwalls*
Flowers: *Mid-June to July*
Status: *Uncommon in limited habitat; endangered species in Maine; threatened species in New Hampshire*

Mountain Heath *Phyllodoce caerulea*

MOUNTAIN SANDWORT
Minuartia groenlandica

Probably the most common and conspicuous of alpine flowers in New Hampshire's Presidential Range, the mountain sandwort became celebrated among turn-of-the-century tourists who called it mountain daisy and took many samples back down with them after their cog railway or carriage road adventure. One such collection hangs on the wall of a local inn with the legend, "The only Plant Which blooms at the Summit of Mount Washington." It also holds the record for the earliest plant to bloom there, recorded on March 11, 1871.

Fortunately, mountain sandwort thrives in the kind of gravelly, disturbed soils that hiker traffic creates on New England's mountaintops. In fact, here's one plant that seems to prefer the beat-up ground along well-trod trails. Ranging from Greenland to New York, this sandwort grows on the highest peaks of Maine and Vermont, as well as on coastal ledges and mountaintops in Acadia National Park. Blossoms can be found atop Mt. Monadnock on the very same rock unit that composes the summit of Mt. Washington (Littleton schist). The Monadnock plants thrive on what, according to popular report, is the most climbed mountain in America.

Sandworts get their common name and former scientific name (*Arenaria* from *arena*, "sand") from the tendency of some species to grow in sandy places. They are most typical of granitic areas, source of most of the quartz in sand grains. Three rare New England species grow on specialized rock strata. *Minuartia stricta*, rock sandwort, is found on dry, lime rock ledges in the Berkshires, Green Mountains, and rarely in New Hampshire. *M. rubella*, Arctic sandwort, also grows on limy rocks and is found on landslides in Smugglers Notch in Vermont, where it is an endangered species. *M. marcescens*, serpentine sandwort, is rarer still, found in a single location in the United States on a serpentine ledge in the northern Green Mountains.

The sandworts have simple flowers with parts in neatly described groups: five sepals, five petals, ten stamens, three styles. Less simple is the grouping and naming of the plants: most sources still list the genus name *Arenaria*, once preferred by American botanists, whereas general usage now favors the European system of several names, including *Minuartia* for our mountain species. Hikers, delighted by the dense growth of sandwort and its long blooming season, may be forgiven if they simply call it mountain daisy.

Habitat: *Gravelly alpine areas, ledges*
Flowers: *June to September*
Status: *Uncommon*

Mountain Sandwort *Minuartia groenlandica*

MOUNTAIN AVENS
Geum peckii

The five-petaled yellow blossoms of mountain avens are one of the special pleasures of New Hampshire's White Mountains, the only place in the world where this high country show can be seen. A single other station—a raised coastal bog on Brier Island in western Nova Scotia—describes the entire worldwide range of *Geum peckii*. Few truly endemic plants inhabit New England, a result of the established flora being wiped away by ice age glaciers. Species closely related to our mountain avens grow in the Great Smoky Mountains and the north Pacific area, but they are so distant in time and geography as to be distinct from our species.

Mountain avens was first collected during the scientific expedition that explored the Presidential Range in 1804. Prof. William D. Peck of Harvard College brought samples back to Cambridge that year, but the classification was not published until 1811 when F. Pursh named the species for its discoverer.

There are eight New England species of avens, but only half of them have yellow petals and no other occurs above timberline. Superficially resembling a buttercup, the flower is in the typical rose family style, with five showy petals, green sepals below, and numerous stamens and pistils above. The seeds ripen to form a burlike structure, though mountain avens seeds lack the hooked ends that allow lowland species to hitch a ride on fur and feathers. Like other avens, this one has divided leaves, though close examination is needed to notice the smaller leaflets below the large, kidney-shaped toothed leaflets at the ends of the stalk.

Mountain avens seems almost too large and lush for its surroundings, blooming as it does next to compact mats of diapensia or mountain cranberry. Quite common within its limited habitats in the alpine zone or on ledges beside waterfalls at lower elevations (where the seeds may have been washed down from above), mountain avens is a fitting symbol of the wildflower heritage of the Granite State.

Habitat: *Wet ledges and alpine lawns*
Flowers: *June to August*
Status: *Rare; New Hampshire only, and there a threatened species*

Mountain Avens   *Geum peckii*

MOUNTAIN GOLDENROD
Solidago macrophylla

Goldenrods are prodigious flower producers. The scores of roadside species spread their yellow clouds across the late-summer landscape to the delight of bees and the bane of misinformed humans, who falsely accuse the flowers of causing hay fever. This undeserved reputation is a result of a botanical case of guilt by association because at the same time that the goldenrod makes such a show, the inconspicuous green flowers of ragweed open and cast their irritating pollen grains to the winds. Only 1 or 2 percent of airborne pollen comes from goldenrods. The flowers, adapted to insect pollination, produce large, sticky pollen grains, incapable of causing distress to the human respiratory system.

Certainly the most widespread and easily recognized group of plants in the Northeast, the individual goldenrod species are difficult to identify when massed by the roadside. Mountain goldenrod, also known as large-leaf goldenrod, is far easier to identify than most, both by its character and its habitat. The stem leaves definitely deserve their Latin name *macrophylla* ("large leaf") as they are both broad and long (to 3 by 4 inches), with a rounded base and conspicuous wings along the leaf stalk. An indicator plant of the Canadian Zone forest, mountain goldenrod is common along the trails of northern New England at all elevations. The plant's occurrence is spotty to the south, hopscotching down to Mt. Greylock by way of outlying peaks like Ascutney, Sunapee, and Monadnock.

In alpine areas mountain goldenrod grows in sheltered sites where soil and water support the nutrient needs of a plant of its size. The flowers of this species are much larger than most other woodland goldenrods, with a conspicuous difference in the size of ray and disk flowers. On Katahdin, Washington, and Mansfield one may find the variety *thyrsoidea* with even larger flower heads than normal, consisting of up to 100 florets rather than the typical 30. The krummholz-protected edges of the Alpine Garden are a good place to look for both the typical mountain goldenrod and the variety.

The genus name for goldenrods, *Solidago*, means "to make whole [or solid]," a reference to an early use in healing wounds. Unfortunately, the only cure for the hurt caused by the appearance of the first goldenrod—farewell summer—is the arrival of another mountain spring, after a long six-month wait.

Habitat: *Moist mountain slopes*
Flowers: *July through September*
Status: *Common in northern New England; threatened species in Massachusetts*

✓Mountain Goldenrod   *Solidago macrophylla*

ALPINE RATTLESNAKE ROOT
Prenanthes boottii

This inconspicuous alpine plant, endemic to the northeastern United States, deserves a better name. Rattlesnake root signifies its use in treating snakebites—a use no alpine traveler in New England will ever need. The tuberous roots of the plants are said to be "intensely bitter" and were brewed into a tonic used to treat dysentery. The group's more descriptive Greek name—*Prenanthes*—is translated as "drooping blossom," in reference to the downward-facing flowers, unusual in the composite family.

This species recalls its discoverer, John W. Boott, who first collected it in the White Mountains in 1829. Later, William Peck collected it from Mt. Marcy in New York. (In his study of alpine plants in that state, Peter Zika postulates that Peck's collection of five plants may have led to the loss of the station: a lesson to modern trowel-wielders.) The plant is not uncommon in the Presidential Range, but has few sites beyond that. In Maine three mountains, including Katahdin, harbor it; in Vermont two, including a Mt. Mansfield station far below timberline. Two New York sites complete the world's range of Boott's rattlesnake root, a candidate for federal listing as an endangered species.

Of three species of *Prenanthes* growing in alpine areas, this is the smallest in stature but has the largest and most showy flowers, a common trait of alpine plants. Despite the Greek name, many of alpine rattlesnake root's flowers are erect and they are conspicuously whiter than the blossoms of the other two species (which tend to a cream color). To cop your identification, count the flat ray flowers (or ligules) in each head—this species will usually have more than a dozen, the others fewer.

Of the other two species, the tall white lettuce (*Prenanthes altissima*) is rarely found in the alpine zone. The dwarf rattlesnake root (*Prenanthes trifoliata*) is an important alpine plant in its own right. In fact, in Maine it is classified as endangered, a higher ranking than the alpine species. Low growing, with nodding cream-colored flowers, the dwarf rattlesnake root blooms a bit later than its alpine cousin, but shares the same high summer meadows and streamsides.

Habitat: *Alpine meadows, fellfields, streambanks*
Flowers: *Late July to August*
Status: *Rare; highest mountains only; candidate species for federal listing; endangered in Vermont; threatened in Maine and New Hampshire*

Alpine Rattlesnake Root *Prenanthes boottii*

ARNICA
Arnica lanceolata

Appreciation of this sunflower-like plant, also known as *Arnica mollis*, is heightened by some knowledge of plant geography. The leafy clumps of arnica, topped with bright yellow flower heads in breezy bouquets, are typical of our highest mountain ravines in August. But midsummer displays of arnica are also in the floral character of the Rockies, where a number of similar species are found. Out there amateur botanists bemoan the DYCs (damned yellow composites), which cause so much confusion in identification. Here, only arnica opens yellow, daisy-shaped flower heads to make connections to mountains on the other side of the Great Plains.

During the summer flowering peak, composite flowers carpet the country from New England ravines to Colorado meadows. Composites are one of the largest plant families in variety of species and number of individuals. Their novel flower design is a composite head of disk flowers and/or showy ray flowers. The most widespread and well-known composite of our time is the dandelion, composed of only ray flowers. Sharing the gaudy yellow color and the same bristly seed head (the pappus), the dandelion and arnica have another peculiarity in common.

Most flowers require pollination and fertilization to produce seed. The pollen, containing the male cells, eventually grows to merge with the egg, leading to the formation of seed in the sharing of genetic information. Arnica, like the dandelion, has no use for this process. Although the ray and tube flowers of the arnica have the required parts, they do make use of sexual reproduction. Instead, in a process called apomixis, no true egg or sperm cells are produced and the seed develops on its own, direct from the parent. Each seed is, in fact, a vegetative clone.

The European species of arnica has long been used in medicine to reduce swelling—a fact that would have been useful to the naturalist Thoreau when he took a bad fall in Tuckerman Ravine, sprained an ankle, and, at the same time, found his first arnica flower.

Habitat: *Moist alpine areas, streamsides*
Flowers: *July and August*
Status: *Rare; threatened species in New Hampshire; special concern*
    species in Maine; believed to be extirpated in Vermont

Arnica   *Arnica lanceolata*

ALPINE GOLDENROD
Solidago cutleri

First described by M. L. Fernald in 1908, alpine goldenrod is restricted to the mountains of the northeastern United States, from Katahdin to the Adirondacks. Although it has been reported from a few low-altitude locales, where its parachute-like seeds might have drifted onto its preferred habitat of gravelly soils, it is an indicator plant of our alpine tundra—*the* goldenrod most likely to be encountered in the open areas of our highest mountains. Fernald named the plant in honor of Manasseh Cutler (1742–1823), a Massachusetts clergyman and naturalist who botanized in the Presidential Range in 1784 and 1804.

Seldom growing over 6 inches high, with but a few leaves on its solitary or tufted flowering stems, alpine goldenrod does just what you'd expect of a highland plant: it hunkers down and hugs the warm and protective earth, without giving up the upright stance of the goldenrod clan.

There are plenty of goldenrods growing in North America—around 100 depending on who's counting—but only a few in other parts of the world. The confusion of species is compounded by their ability to hybridize.

In the mountains *Solidago cutleri* can cross with another northern species, *S. glutinosa*, producing intermediate forms. Rand's goldenrod is not uncommon on lower ledges, but only occasionally ventures above tree line. The best way to distinguish the two is by stem (up to 2 feet tall and sometimes empurpled in *S. glutinosa*) and leaves. The leaves of alpine goldenrod seldom number more than seven on each stem, these being only slightly smaller than the basal leaves. Rand's goldenrod leaves number up to 20 per stem and are noticeably smaller than the basal leaves. The taxonomy of the goldenrods is in a constant state of flux. The artificial grouping by color is being challenged by modern botanists who now include some small white asters in the genus *Solidago*, where until now only the cream-colored silver rod broke the color line.

The English species of goldenrods are called farewell summer. The sentiment is appropriate to the alpine goldenrod, appearing as summer prepares to make its early exit from the mountains. You may very well view alpine goldenrod in an early September ice storm. What a relief the abundant nectar and pollen of the goldenrod flowers is to the bees and butterflies that survive into the alpine version of Indian summer.

Habitat: *Alpine tundra*
Flowers: *Late July to September*
Status: *Rare; threatened species in New Hampshire;*
    special concern species in Maine

Alpine Goldenrod   *Solidago cutleri*

PALE PAINTED CUP
Castilleja septentrionalis

Northern New England's premier peaks—Katahdin, Washington, Mansfield—harbor colonies of this "northern" (the meaning of *septentrionalis*) relative of the Indian paintbrushes so common in Rocky Mountain meadows. While naturalists struggle to differentiate the 200 species of western paintbrushes, we have an easy time with but one species in our mountains. The only other New England species is the scarlet painted cup of southern woods and meadows.

The genus was named in honor of a Spanish botanist, Domingo Castillejo, by a colleague who found the plant in Colombia. New Hampshire's species of *Castilleja* was noted by the first scientific party to explore Mt. Washington in July 1784. The Reverend Manasseh Cutler of Ipswich, Massachusetts, wrote the description of "a vegetable resembling narcissus in the bloom, later described as like a tulip and identified as *Bartsia pallida*." Although the plant proved to be of a genus other than *Bartsia* (a single species of which occurs in arctic America), the *pallida* species name has been used as a synonym for this plant.

The pallid, cream-colored upper leaves, sometimes tinged with bronze or purple or even red, are best referred to as floral bracts. Flowers in the painted cups are compact and inconspicuously colored, relying on the attractive power of the bracts to lure pollinators. The only part of the flower that rises above the bracts is the pistil. To view the rest, push the bracts gently aside. You'll find a reduced version of the standard snapdragon family flower: the three-lipped lower petal reduced to a slight appendage, the upper two-lobed petal keeled and overthrust in a kind of miniature bird's beak. There's so little room inside the flower that the stamens are arranged in ranks and the anthers elongated to fit in the narrow space.

On Mt. Washington the plant grows in handsome colonies on the headwalls of the ravines, where running water minimizes the acidity of the soils. Like all members of the genus, this is believed to be a partial root parasite, depending on other plants for vital nutrients and water. The root system is reduced, composed largely of structures called haustoria, elongate tubes that attach to the roots of the host plant.

Though the colors of painted cups suggest they be planted in gardens, the need for a specific host plant precludes much success. Naturally tended alpine gardens are the best place to enjoy the unusual beauty of pale painted cup.

Habitat: *Alpine ravines and notches*
Flowers: *July to August*
Status: *Rare; threatened species in Vermont and New Hampshire*

Pale Painted Cup   *Castilleja septentrionalis*

Non-native lupine meadow, New Hampshire

ALIEN SPECIES

Plants have adapted to all of the earth's environments, and each species has a particular means of dispersal. Seeds come in a wide range of shapes and sizes, sharing the single purpose of renewing the species' gene pool. To do so, new ground must be found. Maple samaras fly through the air like whirling helicopter blades, dandelion seeds float on gossamer parachutes, beggar-ticks stick to pants legs and animal fur, fruit seeds are prepared for germination in their passage through animal guts. Enormous coconuts float across the world's oceans, while orchid seeds as fine as dust are carried across continents by the wind.

In New England many of our most familiar wildflowers originated in seeds purposely or accidentally brought to this country by European settlers. In grain sacks, in garden seed packets, on worn satchels, and stuck in shoe leather came the seeds that had shared the immigrants' Old World fields. The pernicious weed plantain is such an immediate follower of European colonists that it has been called white man's foot, springing up wherever he steps.

Many alien plant species of European and Asian origin have become established and appreciated components of our flora. Tropical imports have fared poorly in our harsh climate, though global warming promises to allow more southern species to enter our area, to the possible detriment of native plants. Our wealth of roadside flowers would be impoverished without these flowers so suited to disturbed and cultivated areas. New England's native flora was adapted to a forest habitat, with relatively few species living in rich, grassy meadows along river bottoms or on dry, open ridges.

The environments created during the European conquest of our landscape were gardens, fields, pastures: inhospitable to trout lily, bunchberry, and lady's-slipper. These woodland plants retreated before the plow, surviving in remnant woodlots and the wilder mountain country, then returning to the second-growth lowland forests. In sunny, grass-dominated roadsides the foreigners—buttercup, daisy, devil's paintbrush—still find their preferred habitat. Dandelions blooming about mountain campsites attest

171

to the superior ability of these plants to hitch a ride on hikers. A dwarf snapdragon is found growing in the rocky railroad beds that mimic its native habitat.

Unfortunately, many introduced species of plants are opportunists that capitalize on a variety of environments, including the last strongholds of rare species. The resemblance to the sordid history of settlers displacing Native Americans is painfully apt: there's sad irony in the designation of wildflower "reservations." The honeysuckles are a good example of this floral version of Manifest Destiny; both shrub and vine species of Eurasian origin are prevalent where native plants once grew. Accidental or planned, introductions can go awry: the purple bloom of loosestrife in New England wetlands is a colorful banner of an environmental dilemma. Where once diversity was the rule, a monoculture now dominates.

Still, there are alien species of plants that have a more benign character. Scores of intriguing species were planted for their ornamental beauty in the gardens and dooryards of hill-country farms. In places these garden plants are persistent (as the lilac growing in a forest opening), in other places they are accidental (as in the fennel plant that pops up along a roadside). The plants described in this chapter can be considered naturalized, that is, growing on their own as if wild, as the helleborine orchid does.

So, here we spotlight six species that add interest and beauty to the mountain landscapes of New England. Some of these plants, like the garden lupine, have become almost emblematic of high country meadows. Others share the status of rarities with native plants, having strictly defined habitat requirements. In common with the native wildflowers described throughout this book, they are unusual and eye-catching, and have something to say about the health of our regional environment. All of these species, for the moment, are intriguing additions to our floral melting pot or, more accurately, our floral mosaic.

COLTSFOOT
Tussilago farfara

During the grim, interminable mud season of early spring, welcome sights along roadside ditches and cut banks are the sunny yellow heads of coltsfoot. While superficially resembling the dandelion, another yellow composite that flowers about the same time, coltsfoot is a far more interesting plant.

Rising from a fleshy rhizome, this perennial native of Eurasia and North Africa sports a solitary head of yellow disk and ray flowers atop a woolly scape or peduncle, lacking true leaves. The fertile ray flowers are pistillate whereas the inner disk flowers are generally male and sterile. Long after the flowers have produced lustrous silken fruits, the large leaves are produced at the base of the flower stem. These roundish leaves look more like a webbed goose foot than its namesake, coltsfoot.

A monotypic genus, this plant has been used for as long as recorded history as a remedy for respiratory problems such as sore throat, coughing, and bronchitis. The leaves and stems do contain a mucilage that has soothing qualities on mucous membranes; the Latin name *Tussilago* is derived from *tussis* for "cough." Alkaloids found in the leaves act as antihistamines, but if taken in too large a dose can affect liver function.

Coltsfoot is almost always found where soils contain a good amount of clay, hence its other name, clay-weed. Its medicinal history is also reflected by its many colloquial names such as coughweed and coughwort, as well as the less appropriate dummy-weed.

Habitat: *Cut banks, roadsides, wet clay soils*
Flowers: *March to April*
Status: *Locally common*

Coltsfoot   *Tussilago farfara*

MOSS PHLOX
Phlox subulata

The genus *Phlox* consists of about 60 American species, none of which are native to New England's mountains. Still this species, also known as mountain phlox or ground phlox, has become a familiar part of the up-country spring flower display. Known for its ease of cultivation, moss phlox spreads a green carpet across sandy cut banks. A creeping plant, tough and almost woody at its base, this is a popular species for rock gardens or as front-yard ground cover. Moss phlox is particularly noticeable in old cemeteries, where it spreads through the turf grasses and cheers the somber gravestones with splashes of pink.

The natural range of mountain phlox is from Long Island west to Michigan and south to Maryland, growing on sandy soils in open sun. Southward it grows along the Blue Ridge in exposed, rocky habitats. Like the garden phlox and wild blue phlox, this plant from the South and West was brought to New England for its ornamental value (there are a few reports of the medicinal use of some phlox for digestive ailments), spreading from dooryard to roadside.

Most of our wild material has a pleasing pink color, with some tending toward pale blue. Botanical catalogs offer differing descriptions of the character of the phloxes. An old text calls them "insipid." But the modern garden variety 'Temiscaming' is described as being "shocking, bright magenta-crimson." Funny what a little genetic engineering, and botanical spin control, can do.

The Greek name *phlox* means "flame." Originally this name was applied to a brightly colored member of the genus *Lychnis* of the pink family. Though not closely related, the phlox family shares the five cleft petals found in *Lychnis* and the related genus *Silene*, and so the name transition was easily accomplished. There is, in fact, a superficial resemblance of this moss pink to the moss campion *(Silene acaulis)* of our alpine zone. Although living in different climates, the plants both grow in exposed, low-nutrient habitats. Here the growth form of low, linear-leaved foliage and massed pink flowers serves equally well for unrelated plants. This convergent evolution demonstrates that the character of the surrounding environment exerts selective pressure upon the shape of the organisms living there.

Habitat: *Sandy roadsides, lawns*
Flowers: *May though early June*
Status: *Locally naturalized*

Moss Phlox   *Phlox subulata*

GRECIAN FOXGLOVE
Digitalis lanata

A windshield survey for traveling botanists generally involves the somewhat nervewracking activity of scanning plant growth along the sides of interstates looking for an unusual color or form while still attempting to travel 65 miles an hour in the same lane. It was while navigating Route 7 south of Burlington, Vermont, that we first spotted the large spires of Grecian foxglove towering above the surrounding vegetation.

This wonderfully ornate plant grows to 4 feet and somehow finds the energy to form 40 to 50 tubular flowers on a long, tapering spike. The flowers are fairly typical of other foxgloves, but the color is distinctive, with the bowl-shaped creamy calyx veined in maroon while a snow white lip spills out below. A biennial, its first-year basal rosette of lanceolate leaves erupts in an impressive floral spike in its second, and last, year of life.

As its name implies, Grecian foxglove hails from southeastern Europe, including Greece, Italy, and Turkey. While it can escape from cultivation, it does so much less often than the closely related garden foxglove *(Digitalis purpurea)*. The Ferrisburg, Vermont, station is one of the few populations recorded on a regular basis in the entire New England region.

Grecian foxglove contains the heart stimulant digitalis, a glycoside that in the right dosage can save a life, but if taken in too large a dose can have fatal results.

The foxglove name is derived from folk's glove. In old England the good folks were woodland fairies who would make a gift of the flowers to the fox, who could then tread more stealthily in tracking his unwary quarry while wearing the soft blossoms on its paws. Alphonso Wood's *Fourteen Weeks In Botany* text written in 1879 states, "This plant is still thought by the ignorant to be a favorite lurking place of the fairies." Ignorant indeed!

Habitat: *Roadside ditches*
Flowers: *July to early August*
Status: *Rare and local*

Grecian Foxglove *Digitalis lanata*

GARDEN COLUMBINE
Aquilegia vulgaris

Few plant families exhibit the floral diversity of the buttercups. In common they all have separate sepals, petals, stamens, and pistils. But the shape of the flowers ranges from the simplicity of the buttercup, through the doubled and redoubled appearance of the peony, to the bizarre shapes of larkspur and monkshood.

Also called granny's bonnet or, in Quebec, *gants de Notre Dame*, the common and scientific names of columbine reflect imagination and uncertainty. Columbine derives from *columba*, "the dove." The fanciful resemblance of the flowers to a quintet of doves clustered about a water dish is difficult to explain on paper. Perhaps a bit easier to imagine is the resemblance of the hooked spurs to the talons of the eagle, *aquila*, continuing the avian metaphor. Yet, some sources say that it is the Latin *aqua legere* ("to collect water") that explains the name *Aquilegia*. Although the downward-facing flowers clearly do not *collect* water, they *do* exude nectar.

The extremely specialized floral design of the columbine is an adaptation to ensure pollination. The swept-back spurs of each of the five petals contain sweet nectar coveted by bees, moths, and hummingbirds. In probing the spurs, the nectar collector inevitably dusts itself with pollen from the exserted stamens, carrying the load to the next flower to allow the necessary exchange of genetic information through the pistils.

All this is purely academic to the nectar gatherers that visit columbine flowers. Native wild columbines, with their red petals and long spurs, have an evolutionary design for service by hummingbirds. The garden columbine, evolved in a landscape without hummingbirds, is colored blue, purple, or pink—colors attractive to bees—and has spurs short enough to be reached by insect tongues. Thus, the seemingly strange design of a columbine is an emblem of the interaction of animals and plants.

Bees sometimes shortcut the pollination process by boring into the spurs and lapping up the nectar. Gardeners, with no need for nectar, can be selective about their pollinating. Double flowers can be found even along roadsides, but there are flowers in which the nectar spurs are totally eliminated, leaving a flat flower with a family resemblance to other buttercups.

Habitat: *Roadsides, woods near old settlements*
Flowers: *Late May to June*
Status: *Frequently naturalized*

Garden Columbine   *Aquilegia vulgaris*

GARDEN LUPINE
Lupinus polyphyllus and *L. nootkatensis*

Although introduced into northern New England from the Pacific Northwest, the garden lupine has easily taken a favored place in our floral landscape. Early summer finds whole fields turned blue with spikes of lupine blossoms, offering a perfect foreground for countless snapshots of distant peaks. From its native habitat of moist meadows and woods, these two species have moved through garden plantings into the wild, becoming increasingly common in suitable areas. Jefferson, New Hampshire, seems to be the present lupine capital of the mountain region, but stands are not uncommon in Maine, and roadside plantings are springing up in Vermont.

The name lupine is a perfect springboard for a discussion of the plant's complex ecology. Derived from the Latin word for wolf, the name was bestowed by those who saw the plant growing on poor soil and assumed that it was "devouring" the soil's fertility. In fact, like all members of the legume family, lupine has the exceptional ability to create nitrogen-based nutrients for itself and to enrich the surrounding soils (to the tune of 200 pounds of nitrogen per acre in some legume test plots).

This seemingly magical ability is explained by microscopic examination of the plant's roots where a strain of bacteria called *Rhizobium* is enlisted by the plant to serve its needs. Chemicals released into the soil encourage the growth of free-living bacteria near the roots. Some of these become modified bacteroids and are surrounded by root tissue to form small pink spheres or nodules. (Interestingly, the pink color derives from an organic chemical, leghemoglobin, similar to that which colors our blood red.)

Once the root nodules have formed, the bacteroids use atmospheric nitrogen (N_2) to create other, more useful forms, such as ammonium and amino acids. Root tissues of the plant enter the *Rhizobium* bacteroids and carry these nitrogen compounds to the plant's growth centers. The result is the mass of bloom we find in lupine fields each year, plus all the vegetative growth that eventually finds its way back into the soil.

Poisonous alkaloids make lupine poor feed for cattle and humans. Although Native Americans were said to be able to brew a tea from the seeds, all parts are considered extremely poisonous. The seeds are most interesting for their habit of being popped out of the ripe pods, and for their notoriety as the oldest seeds ever germinated. Paleobotanists found seeds of an arctic lupine believed to be 10,000 years old in an animal burrow. Brought to light, they germinated in two days' time.

Habitat: *Roadbanks, fields*
Flowers: *June and July*
Status: *Locally naturalized in Maine and northern New Hampshire*

Garden Lupine   *Lupinus polyphyllus* and *L. nootkatensis*

HELLEBORINE
Epipactis helleborine

Several years ago we received a call from a woman who wanted an identification made on a plant that had mysteriously appeared in her garden, lawn, and even between the flagstones of her backyard walk. She had never seen the plant in the 20 years she had owned the land. One quick look confirmed the identification; helleborine had spread to yet another location in New England.

Helleborine *is* a mysterious plant. Sometimes growing to a yard in height, it can produce a long, one-sided raceme of up to 50 flowers in an area where it has not been seen before. Disturbance to the substrate in moist wooded areas seems to create ideal habitat for this species, which has the ability to, as Fernald states, "appear as if spontaneous." The hundreds of minute, pollenlike seeds can float on the air for many miles, germinating finally in a site where just the right combination of moisture, light, and disturbance exists.

Helleborine is our area's only non-native orchid. Known for centuries in Eurasia as a curative for gout, helleborine was first discovered in this country by an amateur botanist in Syracuse, New York, in 1879. From there it spread rapidly, as non-natives do, to Massachusetts in 1902, Vermont in 1925, and New Hampshire in 1942. It is now fairly common throughout New England west to the Great Lakes and south to Missouri.

The plant can hardly be dismissed as a weed. Besides its sometimes impressive size, the flowers are an attractive maroon to madder purple. The saccate lip is divided into two sections; the upper hypochile produces loads of nectar, while the lower section, or epichile, provides a kind of ledge or seat for certain small wasps to sit and sip the sweet stuff. The leafy stem somewhat resembles the pleated leaves of the false hellebore *(Veratrum viride)* or lady's-slipper *(Cypripedium* spp.). All in all, it is an impressive and interesting addition to our region's flora.

Habitat: *Wooded areas*
Flowers: *July and August*
Status: *Uncommon, but expanding*

Helleborine   *Epipactis helleborine*

Warning for hikers, Monroe Flats, New Hampshire

RARE AND
ENDANGERED FLOWERS

Throughout this book there has been an emphasis on some of the more unusual wildflowers of New England's mountains. Long an avocation of summer visitors, botany has taken on a *legal* framework only in the past couple of decades. At the federal level the passage of the Endangered Species Act, with its various extensions and revisions, has provided a modicum of protection for a small number of species. State Natural Heritage programs with trained staff now exist in all states, and coordination of a region-wide Plant Conservation Program has begun under the aegis of the New England Wild Flower Society. The Afterword explores human impacts and efforts to save rare species.

What makes a plant rare? Partly it is a matter of human definition. Ask the average resident to name a rare plant and it is likely that you'll hear "pink lady's-slipper." Indeed, in the habitats where most of us spend the day—cities, towns, malls, backyards—this is the case. For years the fiction of "It's against the law to pick one!" was used to inculcate a sense of stewardship (in a negative manner) in children. In New Hampshire the plant is now designated as state wildflower and is listed as a species of special concern. The listing has far more to do with public interest and exploitation than with rarity—in fact, this is one of our most widespread orchids.

On another level, botanists have disagreements over the interpretation of various species based on their genetic identity. Certain scientists may consider New England populations distinct species, whereas others consider them varieties of plants that are common elsewhere. Whether discussed in legislative halls or laboratories, the emphasis on identifying and planning for the preservation of a floral heritage is a matter of human perception and a measure of our concern for biological diversity.

The most obvious New England rarities are those restricted to the alpine zone of our highest peaks. Here relict populations, identical or closely related to plants that are widespread in the arctic, make their last stand in New England—at least until the next ice age. Isolated on these mountain islands (where U.S. Forest Service warning signs advertise "the world's worst weather"), some of these plants are genetically different from their northern relatives. Thus the Robbins' cinquefoil is a White Mountain endemic, limited to two natural populations in New Hampshire's small alpine domain.

Even at lower elevations, habitat is the key to the relative rarity of a wildflower. The second federally endangered species featured here, Jesup's milk vetch, grows in only a few sites along the middle Connecticut River. No obvious distinctions in soil chemistry were noted in some recent tests, but the habitat—rocky banks just above river level—is one that has been heavily impacted by damming of the river along most of its length. Still, the milk vetch was probably never abundant. For whatever reason—changing climate, genetic failure, random distribution—certain flowers are naturally rare. In fact, the building of a dam on the Winooski River led to the extinction of a related variety that grew in that single Vermont locale.

When the habitat is vulnerable or rare to begin with, the plants adapted to life there are candidates for rarity. Other plants have spotty distribution not immediately related to where they grow. Although relatively abundant in certain forest types in upper Michigan, ram's head lady's-slipper is restricted to a few unrelated sites in New England. Calypso orchid, too, is of limited occurrence in New England, primarily in cedar swamps. Yet in the West it is a fairly common forest plant, growing in dry aspen woodlands in the Rockies.

Climate and soils are the natural limits that create biological crossroads in any region. Southern plants follow river valleys to make their northernmost stands here, just as norterly plants occur down the mountain backbone to their most southerly limits. Add a requirement for a particular nutrient not commonly found in the region and you have the situation that makes New England rock cress rare. East-to-west range extensions are far less marked, but there are midwestern components in the flora of the Champlain Valley of Vermont where the Great Lakes province reaches our area.

Finally, there are a few botanical puzzles, well represented by the three birds orchid. Known from only a few scattered locations, this tiny plant blooms at a specific time each year—in mass blooms on particular days. Hundreds of plants may appear one year and only a few the next, as the plants survive underground in nonblooming years. Other orchids, with their fine seeds and specific soil needs, tend to "move around" from year to year. The knowledge that such intricate lifestyles persist in rare and unnoticed plants greatly enriches the pursuit of wildflowers.

DWARF CINQUEFOIL
Potentilla robbinsiana

On a hot mid-June day we arrived on the Monroe Flats below the rocky summits of Mts. Washington and Monroe in search of what has been called New England's rarest plant. Inquiry at the nearby Appalachian Mountain Club hut failed to produce the promised guide, but a U.S. Forest Service ranger agreed to escort us to some blooming plants.

Official signs warn hikers away from the cinquefoil's "critical habitat," less than an acre of windswept gravel terraces on a gentle slope. A low gray stone wall circles the area, discouraging trespass without destroying the alpine aesthetics. By luck or design a few plants thrive just outside the wall, and it was at one of these colonies that we took the accompanying photo. Marvelously tiny, in full bloom and with leaves widely spread, the plants are no larger than a quarter. Traces of soil, caught between a gravel pavement created by centuries of freeze and thaw, support the world's largest concentration of this singular species.

Dwarf cinquefoil is a relative of common lawn weeds, easily distinguished by its size. A relict species, it is related to other arctic and alpine cinquefoils, which once may have been a single species. Today the isolated Presidential Range population is different enough in both physical and genetic characteristics to separate it from its nearest relative.

The cinquefoil has a long history of human interest—and intervention. In his delightful study in *Rhodora* (January 1993), Charles Cogbill describes this history in terms of three eras: discovery (by Thomas Nuttall in 1824, but not described as a species until 1840), collection, and stewardship. Despite the eagerness of late-nineteenth-century collectors (you could buy specimens for ten cents each) the colony thrived in its extremely limited and remote habitat.

Far more threatening than botanists were the Vibram-soled hikers who walked through the colony on the old Crawford Path. Surveys indicated that too many hikers wandered out into the gravel flats, stepping on the plants or disturbing the fragile soils. In 1980 the plant was listed as one of the first federally endangered plants in New England, and in 1983 the trail was relocated. Thus a kind of celebrity status has been afforded this tiny member of our mountain community.

Habitat: *Alpine gravel terraces*
Flowers: *Mid-June*
Status: *Two New Hampshire sites only; endangered species in United States and New Hampshire*

Dwarf Cinquefoil   *Potentilla robbinsiana*

SILVERLING
Paronychia argyrocoma var. *albimontana*

Although related to the garden pinks and waste-ground chickweeds, the silverling looks like no other New England plant. The small, five-sepaled, star-shaped flowers have no petals and are hidden within silvery bracts at the tips of equally hoary foliage consisting of small, linear leaves. Growing singly or in tufted colonies on dry, acid ledges, the silverling has a spotty distribution in the White Mountains of New Hampshire and the Longfellow Mountains of Maine. A single coastal station is found near the mouth of the Merrimack River. An indicator species, three-toothed cinquefoil, which shares the silverling's mountain ledge habitat, also grows in disjunct coastal gravel stations.

Nowhere well known, the genus *Paronychia* has representatives in the southern Appalachians and in the Rocky Mountains. Forest and field species of the genus are annuals, lacking the tufted appearance of silverling. One of these, the forked chickweed, is another regional rarity.

The White Mountain silverling was first reported by pioneering naturalist William Oakes in 1847, and described as a separate variety in 1906. Some early botanical specimens are on file from Vermont locations, but the accompanying information is confusing and there are no current records for that state.

European species of this mountain plant have been known for centuries. The alternative common name of whitlow-wort first appeared in the 1500s (modern authors sometimes use nailwort instead). According to the Doctrine of Signatures the plant's resemblance to hangnails—in the whitish linear leaves and bracts—marked it as a cure for nail troubles, including whitlows or felons. The scientific name derives from the Greek word for whitlow combined with the ancient name of a similarly silvery plant used by healers.

Though the flowers are few, concealed, and insignificant, the plant itself has a great deal of character and is best admired during the bright days of high summer on sloping ledges along a White Mountain trail. One need not have a hangnail to seek out the medicinal qualities of such locales.

Habitat: *Dry granite cliffs and ledges*
Flowers: *July to August*
Status: *Rare; endangered species in Massachusetts; threatened in New Hampshire; special concern in Maine*

Silverling *Paronychia argyrocoma* var. *albimontana*

NEW ENGLAND ROCK CRESS
Braya nova-angliae

Once called *Braya humilus*, this plant's old name has the same derivation as *humility* and *humble*, which are descriptive of the demeanor of one of New England's choice rarities, the rock cress. Occurring only on the high cliffs and talus above Vermont's Lake Willoughby, the plant is reported to have been first collected in 1866 by Horace Mann Jr. The plant continues to draw attention today as a disjunct and distinctive species of a little-studied arctic taxon.

The genus *Braya* was named for the Count de Bray of Rouen. Only two other species are recognized by Fernald in eastern North America, both growing on limestone rocks in northwestern Newfoundland. The typical low rock cress is found from Greenland across Canada to Alaska and Asia, its fuzzy fruit capsule differentiating it from the New England species. Some studies of our plant have suggested six races in North America, including another United States station in Michigan. The classification used here lists the Vermont plants as part of a separate species, *B. nova-angliae*. The best summary of this botanical debate is given by Garrett Crow in his work *New England's Rare, Threatened, and Endangered Plants.*

As a group, *Brayas* are sometimes called mouse cresses, in recognition of the low growth habit and tiny hairs on their leaves. Most noticeable to New England explorers of the plant's unique habitat will be the tiny white flowers with four petals in the cross-shaped pattern of the mustard family and the long, thin fruit pods (siliques) with round seeds nestled inside. Certain microscopic features of the cells in the septum—a dividing wall within the pods—are characteristic of this obscure genus.

Despite its limited occurrence, New England rock cress is fairly abundant at the Vermont station—it can be found on roadside gravels at the base of forested talus slopes—and is not in immediate danger of destruction. Still, it symbolizes the fragile nature of our native plant life in relation to soils, climate, and topography, each blossom an inconspicuous banner of biological diversity.

Habitat: *Calcareous cliffs, talus, gravels*
Flowers: *June to July*
Status: *Two New England locations; threatened species in Vermont*

New England Rock Cress   *Braya nova-angliae*

MILK VETCH
Astragalus robbinsii

North America boasts 400 to 500 species of milk vetch, one of the continent's most bewildering arrays of related plants. Equally bewildering is the derivation of its Greek name *Astragalus*, meaning "ankle bone." Found mostly west of the Mississippi, a number of species—poison vetches—are toxic to livestock. The toxicity results from selective uptake of minerals, such as selenium, from the soil. The disoriented wanderings of cows and horses plagued with blindness and muscular disorders from eating locoweed are blamed on species of *Astragalus* and the closely related genus *Oxytropis*.

Robbins' milk vetch was first discovered in 1829 by James Watson Robbins on a limestone ledge along Vermont's Winooski River. In 1894 a dam was built downstream of the site and the area was flooded. No trace of the plant remains. Meanwhile, two varieties of the plant were discovered: Joseph Blake finding variety *blakei* (also known as var. *minor*), and Henry Jesup discovering variety *jesupi* along the Connecticut River.

Milk vetch bears a superficial resemblance to the weed cow vetch, which sports more colorful flowers and leaf tendrils. Jesup's milk vetch makes up for what it lacks in appearance with a number of dubious honors. It has been named the official town flower of Plainfield, New Hampshire, site of one of the world's three colonies of the plant. It is also one of a very select few plants that has been designated a federally endangered species, and it is probably the most uncommon endemic plant species in New England. Like the Robbins' variety, Jesup's milk vetch could be lost to hydro development along the Connecticut River, where it grows at or just above the high-water line. What's more, studies show that deer have a taste for the plant.

Blake's milk vetch is more common within its limited habitat in Vermont, although a historic site in Maine has apparently been lost. A plant of somewhat drier sites, it thrives on calcareous ledges and talus slopes above Lake Willoughby. Here you can get one of the few roadside views of one of New England's rarest plants.

Habitat: *Calcareous ledges and talus slopes*
Flowers: *May to June*
Status: *Rare; Jesup's: endangered species in United States, New Hampshire, Vermont; Blake's: rare in Vermont and special concern (probably extirpated) species in Maine*

Jesup's Milk Vetch
Astragalus robbinsii
var. *jesupi*

Blake's Milk Vetch   *Astragalus robbinsii* var. *blakei*

THREE BIRDS or NODDING POGONIA
Triphora trianthophora

The diminutive little bird orchid is a cipher to plant ecologists. The species is surprisingly widespread, growing in varied habitats from Guatemala and Panama to its northernmost station in the White Mountains of western Maine. Although it is known from wetland and coniferous forest sites to the south, and although it grows at sites upward of 6,000 feet in the Carolina mountains, New England's populations are confined to beech forests at relatively low elevations.

The fragile and somewhat succulent plants emerge from underground tubers, developing in areas of beech leaf mold and beside rotting logs. The plants are believed to take some nourishment from the decaying forest litter, a saprophytic character they would share with other small woodland orchids. Spreading by underground runners, the plants grow in large colonies (one New Hampshire station reportedly had some 10,000 plants). However, emergence of three birds orchids is an irregular occurrence, with abundant blooms one year and only a scattering the next. Thus, the business of finding the flowers of three birds can be like chasing phantoms.

The flowers, as both the common and scientific names imply, usually appear in threes. Still, one to six flowers have been found on some stems, and not all the flowers of a plant bloom at the same time. The matter of flowering in three birds is perhaps its most intriguing aspect. Phillip Keenan reports that the populations he has studied bloom on only five or six days of a month-long season. What's more, the Maine, New Hampshire, and Massachusetts colonies in one year bloomed on the *very same* five days. This unusual floral synchronicity is believed to be an adaptation to ensure cross-pollination between flowers of different plants. (We wonder how much of this precious pollination time was lost on the day when we first saw this flower—in a torrential downpour that must have deterred even the most nectar-addicted insect.)

About 20 stations of this puzzling little orchid are known in New England. Located in low montane forests at the very edge of a much more widespread North American range, these colonies offer a glimpse of evolution at work. *Triphora* could be fertile scientific ground for a budding Darwin lucky enough to arrive during a blooming year on a blooming day.

Habitat: *Beech forests*
Flowers: *August to early September*
Status: *Rare; endangered species in Massachusetts; threatened in Maine, New Hampshire, and Vermont*

Three Birds or Nodding Pogonia *Triphora trianthophora*

RAM'S HEAD LADY'S-SLIPPER
Cypripedium arietinum

"Curious" is how the nineteenth-century botany professor Alphonso Wood described the ram's head lady's-slipper. And curious it is for several reasons. There is no other lady's-slipper in New England smaller or more secretive. Growing scarcely taller than 10 to 12 inches, ram's head's maroon or madder-colored sepals and pouch offer cryptic coloration difficult to detect.

Unlike other members of the genus, the slipper pouch is angled down to a kind of conical point; the entire flower if viewed at a right angle looks like the head of a charging ram. The slipper is delicately laced with maroon veining and has a small, circular opening fringed in white "fur" leading to the nectary and column. Only smaller bees, not the usual bumblebee, can fit into the tiny opening.

Usually seen in northern white cedar *(Thuja)* swamps, this species can also be found along wooded roadsides with moist soil and partial shade. One colony in central Vermont is within a logged area and roadside shoulder, perhaps indicating that ram's head is inured to considerable disturbance.

Ram's head lady's-slipper is rare throughout its range, which covers the northern tier of states from Maine to Minnesota. It is barely hanging on in Massachusetts and New Hampshire and is listed as threatened in Vermont. It thrives in one area of the country, Isle Royale National Park in northern Michigan, where it grows by the hundreds under coniferous overhangs in old dunes.

Habitat: *Cedar swamps, dry forest sites*
Flowers: *May to June*
Status: *Rare; endangered species in Massachusetts and New Hampshire; threatened species in Maine and Vermont; extinct in Connecticut*

Ram's Head Lady's-Slipper   *Cypripedium arietinum*

CALYPSO
Calypso bulbosa var. *americana*

Imagine a cold northern New England white cedar bog, a dark mossy place in early May. Then think of this lilliputian beauty amidst the moxie plum and twinflower, perhaps growing from a rotting cedar log. The first calypso is always a memorable event for the orchid fancier; is it any wonder that the great naturalist John Muir, upon seeing it for the first time, wept at its beauty?

Named for the elusive sea nymph of Homer's *Odyssey*, calypso is the flower world's answer to a Fabergé egg: an exquisite miniature with detail and color startling to behold. The solitary flower is held aloft atop a delicate scape, with five translucent magenta sepals and petals crowning an intricately designed slipperlike pouch. The pouch, actually a modified petal, broadens distally into a snow white apron mottled with madder purple, adorned with three rows of golden yellow bristles resembling pseudo-anthers. All of this marvelous detail in a flower no more than 1 inch long.

The golden runway of bristles leads into the interior of the pouch, an ostensible signpost of a nectar cache for any potential pollinator such as the bumblebee willing to struggle into the slipper. Alas, it is all a shell game; no nectar rewards the inquisitive bee in calypso. The empty promise of the fairy slipper may explain its relatively rare seed capsule formation, at least in the eastern variety (var. *americana*). The plant reproduces more commonly from its coral-like rhizomes and round corm, sending up a single basal leaf in autumn, which overwinters and then withers prior to flowering in early spring.

Despite its delicate appearance, calypso is found in all of the world's coldest climates. Its presence in Lapland, northern Russia and Siberia, as well as Canada and Alaska, makes it a truly cosmopolitan circumboreal species. Calypso reaches its southern range limit in northern New England, where its numbers have been in decline for many years.

Habitat: *Northern white cedar swamps*
Flowers: *Mid-May to June*
Status: *Rare; endangered species in New Hampshire; threatened species in Vermont*

Calypso   *Calypso bulbosa* var. *americana*

Mt. Chocorua, New Hampshire

AFTERWORD:
THREATS ON HIGH

Wearily ascending the Bee-line Trail to Mt. Chocorua in Tamworth, New Hampshire, one hot day, in quest of the rare subalpine species silverling, we were confronted with the dispiriting sight of scores of hikers crowded onto the rocky summit. Mindful of the fact that we all had the gumption to climb a mountain rather than sit by the backyard barbecue, it still saddened us that the wistful notion of mountaintops as remote places of quiet solitude has been irrevocably shattered. The armies of hikers who trek through the rare rock gardens of Washington, Mansfield, Monadnock, and even distant Katahdin are in danger of loving the alpine areas of New England to death.

In an effort to preserve the most vulnerable of New England's rarest plant species, the New England Plant Conservation Program (NEPCoP), a voluntary consortium of 67 private organizations and government agencies, has created a set of regional policies designed to protect the most vulnerable 400 species found in New England. The culmination of this effort will be the *Flora Conservanda*, a list of New England's rarest species both regionally and globally.

The New England Wild Flower Society, as administrative hub of the program, coordinates activities with endangered species task forces from the six states, whose members include representatives from the state Natural Heritage programs, the Center for Plant Conservation, The Nature Conservancy, U.S. Fish and Wildlife Service, and various universities and land trusts. Representatives of these groups decide on a yearly basis which species are most in need of and responsive to protection efforts. There are four basic protocols for preserving rare plant species.

1. Habitat protection and management. The most efficient and successful method to preserve rare plants is through careful monitoring and timely protection against adverse impacts in situ, or within existing natural habitat. This may not always be possible however as, sadly, many private landowners are suspicious of regulators who threaten their inalienable right to do what they want on their own land. The NEPCoP relies completely on voluntary actions, and is not a regulatory program. Since most rare plant habitat in New England is on private lands, tact, patience, and education are essential.

2. Seed banking. If in situ protection is not possible, then an ex situ strategy is followed. Seeds from the wild are collected and preserved to provide an emergency backup in case of catastrophic loss of natural habitat.

3. Living collections. Botanical gardens can preserve genetic material through propagation of rare species in labs and greenhouses. The Garden in the Woods in Framingham, Massachusetts, is the best known of these propagation centers. Although this is an expensive and labor-intensive method to save endangered species, it provides scientific research opportunities and public education potential.

4. Introduction/reintroduction. If a species of plant no longer exists in an area, has been recently extirpated, or its habitat has been altered beyond its carrying capacity, reintroduction may be a suitable solution. Or if suitable habitat exists elsewhere, the plant may be introduced there, as has been done with dwarf cinquefoil in the White Mountains. Both of these techniques have had spotty success and are experimental. Obviously, close monitoring and preservation of existing habitat is the best long-range solution.

Why give a damn about rare plants? Surely saving bald eagles, pandas, and blue whales has captured the public's imagination, while the Furbish lousewort became something of an object of disdain. There are practical reasons we should preserve plants.

- Thirty percent of all modern pharmaceuticals are derived from plants. Such well-known medicines include digitoxin, a cardiac stimulant derived from foxglove; vinblastine, an antileukemia agent from the rosy periwinkle; and taxol, from the Pacific yew, a recent discovery effective against ovarian cancer. If we lose an obscure rush or sedge, will a possible cure for AIDS be gone forever?

- Biodiversity is our most underappreciated but important resource, according to scientist Edward O. Wilson, writing in his landmark book *The Diversity of Life.* The very health and vigor of our own species is dependent on the diversity of the many life forms around us. The successful and healthy functioning of ecosystems is predicated on a diverse and broad-based community approach to land management. Think of it as a barometer of the health of living things: a kind of canary in the mine early warning system.

The loss of a plant species and its unique genetic contribution lead to a loss of dependent animal species, which leads to a breakdown of the ecosystem and eventually to a degraded biosphere. No longer do environmentalists feel that preserves or protected enclaves for a single rare species are effective management options; keeping intact guilds, communities, and unsegmented habitats across political boundaries is the aim of the new environmentalist.

• The preservation, or at least the deceleration of loss, of rare species habitat is imperative to the quality of our lives. Rare plants are interesting, scientifically instructive, and often beautiful. Our lives would be less rewarding if our relations with nature were dictated purely by short-term self-interest. Whether it's the spotted owl or the Furbish lousewort, what gives us the right to accept their demise and to deprive future generations of their existence?

As stewards of the land, we have put financial and recreational benefits ahead of the protection of our wards, the plants and animals who share the planet with us. It makes perfect sense from a practical as well as moral perspective to recognize where we have historically blundered and to change our way of thinking in ecological preservation and management.

STATE LISTS
OF
ENDANGERED WILDFLOWERS

What is rare in one state may be relatively common in another. The following list is a compendium of those wildflower species officially listed as endangered by each state's agency administering a Natural Heritage program or state endangered species law. These are the rarest of the rare, some existing in only a single documented site or of historical occurrence only. Species with an asterisk are considered among the 100 rarest regional species listed in Garrett Crow's 1982 survey, *New England's Rare, Threatened, and Endangered Plants*. Species followed by a double asterisk are also listed as endangered by the federal government. Only wildflowers likely to occur within the area of coverage for this book are listed; grasslike plants, ferns, trees, and shrubs are omitted. **Boldface** species are included in this work.

MAINE

Alleghany Vine	*(Adlumia fungosa)*
Alpine Azalea	***(Loiseleuria procumbens)****
Alpine Bistort	*(Polygonum viviparum)**
Alpine Bitter-cress	*(Cardamine bellidifolia)**
Alpine Marsh Violet	*(Viola palustris)*
Alpine Speedwell	*(Veronica wormskjoldii)*
Arctic Sandwort	*(Minuartia rubella)**
Cut-leaved Toothwort	*(Dentaria laciniata)*
English Sundew	*(Drosera anglica)**
Giant Rattlesnake Plantain	*(Goodyera oblongifolia)*
Lance-leaved Draba	*(Draba lanceolata)**
Lapland Rosebay	***(Rhododendron lapponicum)****
Linear-leaf Sundew	*(Drosera linearis)**
Moss Plant	***(Cassiope hypnoides)****
Mountain Honeysuckle	*(Lonicera dioica)*
Northern Meadowsweet	*(Spiraea septentrionalis)*
Oakes' Eyebright	*(Euphrasia oakesii)**
Prairie White-fringed Orchid	*(Platanthera leucophaea)**
Star Saxifrage	*(Saxifraga stellaris* var. *comosa)**
White Adder's Mouth	*(Malaxis brachypoda)*

209

MASSACHUSETTS

Black Snakeroot	*(Cimicifuga racemosa)*
Broad Waterleaf	*(Hydrophyllum canadense)*
Douglas' Cress	*(Cardamine douglassii)*
Downy Woodmint	*(Blephilia ciliata)*
Dwarf Rattlesnake Plantain	*(Goodyera repens)*
False Pennyroyal	*(Trichostema brachiatum)*
Hairy Beardtongue	*(Penstemon hirsutus)*
Hairy Honeysuckle	*(Lonicera hirsuta)*
Hairy Woodmint	*(Blephilia hirsuta)*
Hooded Ladies-tresses	*(Spiranthes romanzoffiana)*
Mountain Cranberry	***(Vaccinium vitis-idaea)***
Narrow-leaved Vervain	*(Verbena simplex)*
Nodding Chickweed	*(Cerastium nutans)*
Northern Bedstraw	*(Galium boreale)*
Pink Wintergreen	*(Pyrola asarifolia)*
Puttyroot	*(Aplectrum hyemale)*
Ram's Head Lady's-slipper	***(Cypripedium arietinum)*** *
Rand's Goldenrod	*(Solidago glutinosa* var. *randii)*
Sand Violet	*(Viola adunca)*
Sessile Water-speedwell	*(Veronica catenata)*
Small Whorled Pogonia	*(Isotria medeoloides)* **
Small Yellow Lady's-slipper	***(Cypripedium parviflorum)***
Snowberry	*(Symphoricarpos albus)*
Spurred Gentian	*(Halenia deflexa)*
Three Birds	***(Triphora trianthophora)***
Wild Senna	*(Cassia hebecarpa)*

NEW HAMPSHIRE

Alpine Bitter-cress	*(Cardamine bellidifolia)* *
Alpine Brook Saxifrage	*(Saxifraga rivularis)* *
Alpine Speedwell	*(Veronica wormskjoldii)*
Arethusa	*(Arethusa bulbosa)*
Auricled Twayblade	*(Listera auriculata)* *
Baked Apple Berry	*(Rubus chamaemorus)*
Beggar's-lice	*(Hackelia deflexa* var. *americana)*
Butterwort	*(Pinguicula vulgaris)*
Calypso	***(Calypso bulbosa)*** *
Canadian Germander	*(Teucrium canadense* var. *virginicum)*
Carolina Cranesbill	*(Geranium carolinianum)*
Case's Ladies'-tresses	*(Spiranthes casei)*
Cut-leaved Toothwort	*(Dentaria laciniata)*
Dwarf Cinquefoil	***(Potentilla robbinsiana)*** * **
Green Dragon	*(Arisaema dracontium)*
Hairy Rock-cress	*(Arabis hirsuta* var. *pycnocarpa)*
Hound's Tongue	*(Cynoglossum boreale)*
Jesup's Milk Vetch	***(Astragalus robbinsii* var. *jesupi)*** * **
Labrador Bedstraw	*(Galium labradoricum)*

Lance-leaved Draba	*(Draba lanceolata)* *
Large-flowered Bellwort	**(Uvularia grandiflora)**
Leafy-bracted Aster	*(Aster crenifolius* var. *arcuans)*
Livelong Saxifrage	*(Saxifraga aizoon* var. *neogaea)* *
Marsh Valerian	*(Valeriana uliginosa)* *
Mountain Cudweed	*(Gnaphalium supinum)* *
Mountain Sweet-cicely	*(Osmorhiza chilensis)*
Musk Flower	**(Mimulus moschatus)**
Narrow-leaved Cotton Grass	*(Eriophorum angustifolium)*
Nodding Saxifrage	*(Saxifraga cernua)* *
Oakes' Eyebright	*(Euphrasia oakesii)* *
Pale Early Violet	*(Viola affinis)*
Perfoliate Bellwort	*(Uvularia perfoliata)*
Pink Wintergreen	*(Pyrola asarifolia)*
Prickly Rose	*(Rosa acicularis)*
Ram's Head Lady's-slipper	**(Cypripedium arietinum)** *
Robinson's Hawkweed	*(Hieracium robinsonii)*
Rock Sandwort	*(Minuartia stricta)*
Showy Lady's-slipper	**(Cypripedium reginae)**
Sibbaldia	*(Sibbaldia procumbens)*
Small Yellow Lady's-slipper	**(Cypripedium parviflorum)**
Snowy Aster	*(Aster ptarmicoides)*
Spurred Gentian	*(Halenia deflexa)*
Sweet Coltsfoot	*(Petasites frigidus)*
Upland Boneset	*(Eupatorium sessilifolium)*
Water-stargrass	*(Heteranthera dubia)*

VERMONT

Auricled Twayblade	*(Listera auriculata)* *
Boott's Rattlesnake Root	**(Prenanthes boottii)** *
Diapensia	**(Diapensia lapponica)** *
Douglas' Knotweed	*(Polygonum douglasii)*
Drummond's Rock-cress	*(Arabis drummondii)*
Early Thimbleweed	*(Anemone multifida)*
Elm-leaved Goldenrod	*(Solidago ulmifolia)*
Goldenseal	*(Hydrastis canadensis)*
Hairy Pinweed	*(Lechea villosa)*
Hoary Mountain Mint	*(Pycnanthemum incanum)*
Jesup's Milk Vetch	**(Astragalus robbinsii** var. **jesupi)** * **
Large-bracted Tick-trefoil	*(Desmodium cuspidatum)*
Lesser Pyrola	*(Pyrola minor)*
Marsh Valerian	*(Valeriana uliginosa)* *
New England Rock Cress	**(Braya nova-angliae)** *
Pinedrops	*(Pterospora andromedea)*
Prickly Rose	*(Rosa acicularis)*
Sessile-leaved Boneset	*(Eupatorium sessilifolium)*
Southern Twayblade	*(Listera australis)* *
Woodland Cudweed	*(Gnaphalium sylvaticum)*

GLOSSARY

adventive. Non-native plant recently established in area

anthers. Pollen-bearing structures

axil. Point where leaf or leaf stem joins the main stem

bract. A modified leaf, sometimes colored

calyx. The sepals collectively; outer flower part, often green

circumpolar. Species with a world-circling northern or southern range

composite. A flower with ray and/or disc flowers

cordate. Heart-shaped, referring to leaf shape

corm. An enlarged underground stem

corolla. Inner flower part, usually colored

corymb. A flat-topped flower cluster

culm. The stem of a sedge or grass plant

endangered. Legal term for a plant in danger of extinction

ephemeral. Existing for a short period of time

exserted. Projecting beyond an enclosing organ or part

hybrid. A plant created by cross-breeding of species

inflorescence. A cluster of flowers

introduced. A non-native plant

lagg. A ring of open water around a bog

naturalized. A non-native plant that is widespread and well established

ovary. Organ of flower containing ovules, or eggs

ovate. Egg-shaped in outline

perfoliate. A leaf base that surrounds the main stem

phytotaxis. Movement of plant material in response to light

pistil. Female organ of a flowering plant

pollen. Carrier of male cells

raceme. A long flower cluster, the flowers with stems

relict. Species remaining from an earlier climate or community

scape. A leafless flowering stem

sepal. Outer flower part, often green

spadix. A floral spike typical in members of the Arum family

spathe. A sheathing, often hoodlike, modified leaf (or bract) in members of the Arum family

special concern. Legal term for plant that could become endangered or threatened

spore. Reproductive structure of many nonflowering plants

stamen. Male organ of a flowering plant

staminodia. Stamens producing no pollen

stigma. Topmost portion of the pistil

stolons. Stems running and rooting from a plant

strophiole. A nonreproductive portion of the seed

style. Narrow part of the pistil

taproot. A root extending directly down from the stem

teratological. An unusual, often bizarre, form of a plant

threatened. Legal term for a plant threatened with endangered status

umbel. A round, umbrella-like flower cluster

Watch List. Legal term for a plant that could become of special concern, threatened or endangered

whorl. An arrangement of leaves around a central point

FOR FURTHER READING

The following books are especially helpful in identifying and understanding the ecological needs of New England's mountain wildflowers:

Bliss, Lawrence C. 1963. *Alpine Zone of the Presidential Range.* Privately published: Urbana, Ill.

Coffey, Timothy. 1993. *The History and Folklore of North American Wildflowers.* Boston: Houghton Mifflin Co.

Crow, Garrett E. 1982. *New England's Rare, Threatened, and Endangered Plants.* Washington, D.C.: U.S. Fish & Wildlife Service, GPO.

Harris, Stuart K., Jean Langenheim, and Frederic Steele. 1977. *AMC Field Guide to Mountain Flowers of New England.* Boston: Appalachian Mountain Club Books.

Johnson, Charles W. 1985. *Bogs of the Northeast.* Hanover, N.H.: University Press of New England.

Kricher, John C. and Gordon Morrison. 1988. *A Field Guide to Eastern Forests* (Peterson Field Guide Series). Boston: Houghton Mifflin Co.

Newcomb, Lawrence. 1977. *Newcomb's Wildflower Guide.* Boston: Little, Brown & Co.

Pease, Arthur Stanley. 1964. *A Flora of Northern New Hampshire.* Cambridge, Mass.: New England Botanical Club.

Seymour, Frank Conkling. 1982. *The Flora of New England.* Phytologia Memoirs 5. Plainfield, N.J.: Harold N. Moldenke and Alma L. Moldenke.

Steele, Frederic L. 1982. *At Timberline: A Nature Guide to the Mountains of the Northeast.* Boston: Appalachian Mountain Club Books.

Zwinger, Ann and Beatrice Willard. 1989. *Land Above the Trees: A Guide to American Alpine Tundra.* Tuscon: University of Arizona Press.

INDEX

Jeff Wallner

Mario J. DiGregorio

ABOUT THE AUTHORS

Jeff Wallner has 20 years of experience in New Hampshire's White Mountains, including work as field education director with the Society for the Protection of New Hampshire Forests, where he supervised the Lost River Nature Garden, a major collection of mountain flowers in the White Mountains. Jeff has also worked in interpretive efforts, programs, and trail guides at Franconia Notch, Mt. Monadnock, Dixville Notch, Wildcat Mountain, and in the Androscoggin Valley. Trained in resource management and environmental communications in Berlin and Keene, New Hampshire, Jeff has traveled widely in New England as park ranger, interpretive naturalist, and environmental educator. His hobby of "collecting" national parklands has taken him to 345 historic and natural parks in all 50 states and two territories. He is coauthor with Mario J. DiGregorio of the companion volume *A Vanishing Heritage: Wildflowers of Cape Cod.* Jeff currently leads a migratory life as a naturalist at Mesa Verde and Saguaro National Parks.

Mario J. DiGregorio has worked as a park ranger with the National Park Service in Massachusetts, New Jersey, and Colorado and with the Army Corps of Engineers in Illinois and Cape Cod. He was town conservation administrator in Brewster, Massachusetts, and now works as an environmental consultant on Cape Cod where he lives with his wife, Phyllis, and daughter, Sarah. He is a contract field botanist specializing in rare plant preservation for the Massachusetts Natural Heritage and New England Plant Conservation Programs and is coauthor with Jeff Wallner of *Wildflowers of the Cape Cod Canal.* Mario periodically escapes the crush of tourist traffic during the Cape summer to seek safe haven in the mountains of the north country.

We encourage you to patronize your local bookstores. Most stores will order any title that they do not stock. You may also order directly from Mountain Press by mail, using the order form provided below, or by calling our toll-free number and using your Visa or MasterCard. We will gladly send you a complete catalog upon request.

Some other Natural History titles of interest:

____A Guide to Rock Art Sites Southern California and Southern Nevada	$20.00
____Alpine Wildflowers of the Rocky Mountains	$14.00
____Beachcombing the Atlantic Coast	$15.00
____Birds of the Central Rockies	$14.00
____Birds of the Northern Rockies	$12.00
____Birds of the Pacific Northwest Mountains	$14.00
____Coastal Wildflowers of the Pacific Northwest	$14.00
____Edible and Medicinal Plants of the West	$21.00
____Graced by Pines The Ponderosa Pine in the American West	$10.00
____Hollows, Peepers, and Highlands An Appalachian Mountain Ecology	$14.00
____An Introduction to Northern California Birds	$14.00
____An Introduction to Southern California Birds	$14.00
____The Lochsa Story Land Ethics in the Bitterroot Mountains	$20.00
____Mammals of the Central Rockies	$14.00
____Mammals of the Northern Rockies	$12.00
____Mountain Plants of the Pacific Northwest	$20.00
____New England's Mountain Flowers	$17.00
____Northwest Weeds The Ugly and Beautiful Villains of Fields, Gardens, and Roadsides	$14.00
____Owls, Whoo are they?	$12.00
____Plants of Waterton-Glacier National Parks and the Northern Rockies	$12.00
____Roadside Plants of Southern California	$14.00
____Sagebrush Country A Wildflower Sanctuary	$14.00
____Watchable Birds of the Northern Rockies	$14.00
____Watchable Birds of the Southwest	$14.00

Please include $3.00 per order to cover shipping and handling.

Send the books marked above. I enclose $_____

Name_____

Address_____

City_____State_____Zip_____

l Payment enclosed (check or money order in U.S. funds)
Bill my: ☐ VISA ☐ MasterCard Expiration Date:_____

Card No._____

Signature_____

MOUNTAIN PRESS PUBLISHING COMPANY
P.O. Box 2399 • Missoula, MT 59806
Order Toll Free 1-800-234-5308
Have your Visa or MasterCard ready.